Amphibious Spangulatos

or Newt on Your Nellie!

A farce

Paul Doust

Samuel French — London
New York - Toronto - Hollywood

R 69077 W

AMPHIBIOUS SPANGULATOS

Commissioned and first produced by the Watermill Youth Theatre in March 1993. Performed at the Greenwich Theatre, Greenwich, London, on 2nd September 1993, with the following cast:

Cherry Hellingsworth		Anna Francolini
Vanessa Pile		Hannah Waterman
Mother Superior Enid		Alison Chalmers
Dr Barbara Cunningham		Samantha Battersea
Dr Austin Zetanusi		Matt Lucas
Roger Bloom		Gerald Avvakoumides
Gary Alexander	*Cricketers*	Tim Baker
Martin Box		Brendan McNally
Steve Marchant		Mujahid Khan
Mother Superior Millichope		Emma Kilcoyne
Sister Tina		Linda Hall
Sister Pybus		Alison Irvine
Sister Beaverbook		Adele Greensall
Sister Howe		Rebecca Shirley
Sister Litmus		Jennifer Meldrum
Sister Small-Change		Polly Lister
Zandra Emanuel		Kate Ness
Rex Cunningham		Adam Hemming
Keith Block		Graham Avent
Lolita Fenetre		Sophie Garner
Blanche July	*Southern Fried Chickens*	Pauline Hornibrook
Aramist Sweet-Bird II		Polly Tapp
Cyd Spank		Kathryn Ackley
Darren Spavin		Jack Tarlton
Bradley Cabin		Gerald Avvakoumides

Benny Thrower	Daniel Stanley
Bypass Protestors	Joanna Clarke
	Katrina Heath
	Alice Reid
	Rachael Shirley
	Corienda White
Inspector Sheridan	Elliot Levey
PC Carpenter	Carl Sanderson
Inspector Budimir	Tim Nelson

Directed by Edward Wilson
Assisted by Paul Roseby
Designed by Brian Lee
Lighting designed by Jerry Hodgson
Stage Management by Catherine Sherry

CHARACTERS

Cherry Hellingsworth
Vanessa Pile
Dr Barbara Cunningham
Zandra Emanuel
Dr Austin Zetanusi
Rex Cunningham
Keith Block
Chief Inspector Sheridan
PC Carpenter
Inspector Budimir
Mother Superior Enid
Mother Superior Millichope
Sister Tina
Sister Pybus
Sister Beaverbook   } *Sisters*
Sister Howe
Sister Litmus
Sister Small-Change
Roger Bloom
Gary Alexander
Martin Box   } *Cricketers*
Ian Blane
Steve Marchant
Lolita Fenetre
Blanche July
Aramist Sweet-Bird II   } *Southern Fried Chickens*
Cyd Spank
Muriel Yig
Rosalynde Manchester
Darren Spavin
Bradley Cabin
Kirk Maggerty   } *Protesters*
Richard Turnstile
Benny Thrower

Scene — the sports changing room of a village hall
Time — the present

Author's note

If you are able to use more actors (and have the on stage space and resources), then the number of Sisters, Cricketers, Protestors and Southern Fried Chickens can be increased. This will make events such as the "cupboard" gag in Act II even more effective.

Paul Doust

Other plays by Paul Doust
published by Samuel French Ltd:

Cold Comfort Farm
(adapted from the novel by Stella Gibbons)

Lady Bracknell's Confinement

ACT I

The sports changing room of a village hall

There are three doors: X, Y and the storeroom door. Doors X and Y lead off to the rest of the hall. The storeroom door leads nowhere but the storeroom. There are no other entrances or exits. All of these doors get opened, closed and slammed a great deal, so they need to be very secure. There is a shower, which can be represented by a pair of full-length curtains on a rail (the space behind the curtains must be big enough to accommodate a coffin and actors). There is a mirror on the wall next to door X. There is a trolley and a cupboard (large enough to accommodate an actor) which are both on castors. The trolley, which is used to support a coffin, has a cloth around it so that props (and actors) can rest underneath without being seen. The cupboard has a false back, through which actors can pass. One of the walls near door Y has a similar device, as does door X. When the cupboard is placed against the wall or the door, actors can pass straight through, thus effecting the tricks in Act II, described in the text. There is a cricket helmet inside the cupboard. There are several chairs around the edges of the room and two or three around the trolley. Mess is strewn around the room — clothing, sports bags, towels, etc. — the evidence of an absent cricket team

At the opening, door X is wide open, and door Y is closed. The shower curtains are pulled right back

Cherry enters through door Y, carrying a large book. She is extremely anxious. She slams door Y behind her. Noticing that door X is open, she slams it closed. Then she swiftly pulls the shower curtains closed. She paces about, scanning the book and looking horrified

Cherry Oh, what am I going to do? What on earth am I going to do?!

There is a knock at door X. Cherry jumps

   (*Controlling herself*) Stay calm, Cherry—that's what you're going to do. (*She makes for door X, then stops suddenly*)

Another knock

Just a moment! (*She slings the book under the trolley*)

Another knock

Come in!

Vanessa enters from door X

Vanessa Is this the village hall?
Cherry The finest in all the county!
Vanessa But you've put in extra walls.
Cherry You've a keen eye for detail.
Vanessa What do you do here?
Cherry Me? I'm the caretaker.
Vanessa No — what goes on?
Cherry In this hall? Oh, just about everything. This is the changing room. Sports and recreation.
Vanessa Which explains this shower? (*She pulls the shower curtains open*)
Cherry You're nobody's fool. (*She pulls the shower curtains closed*)
Vanessa (*going to the storeroom and opening the door*) Where does this lead to?
Cherry Nowhere. It's the storeroom.

Vanessa closes the storeroom door

We've a lovely main space — but it's taken tonight.
Vanessa Amateur drama?
Cherry Even as we speak, people are watching a play.
Vanessa Fascinating.
Cherry I hope so. Then tomorrow we've got aerobics. We're the centre of the community.
Vanessa I see. A sort of ... Community Centre.
Cherry You could put it like that.
Vanessa I just did.
Cherry Did you? Oh, yes!
Vanessa Are you listening to me?
Cherry Pardon?
Vanessa You look a bit distracted.
Cherry Nothing of the sort! I'm the soul of efficiency! Now, what are you after? Dance? Aromatherapy? Making ornamental knick-knacks out of retired jockeys? We've a very active Protest Group. Are you affected by the bypass? The Protest Group, you see, might be just what you want.

Vanessa It won't come anywhere near me. I live beyond the hill.

Cherry The new development?

Vanessa Yes.

Cherry Then it won't come anywhere near you. So — if you don't want the Protest Group what *do* you want, exactly?

Vanessa I'm depressed and unhappy.

Cherry A listening ear?

Vanessa You're very perceptive.

Cherry My mother was a vet. Please speak freely. I know I can help you. I'm a font of information and I understand everything.

Vanessa Debt counselling.

Cherry Ah, yes. What?

Vanessa Advice for people having problems with money.

Cherry No, I'm sorry — I can't help you.

Vanessa Do you have any rope?

Cherry Why?

Vanessa I'm going to hang myself.

Cherry I see. Well, I think there's some in the nursery area.

Vanessa You keep it for skipping?

Cherry No — for tying up the children. If you'll just wait here ...

Cherry exits through door Y

Vanessa looks up at the ceiling. She sees the shower rail

Vanessa Ah-ha! (*She takes a chair, moves to the shower, pulls back the curtains, places the chair directly under the rail, stands on the chair and pulls at the rail*)

Cherry enters through door X

Cherry Just a minute!

Vanessa Oh!

Cherry Did you say hang yourself!

Vanessa How did you get there? You left by the other one.

Cherry When we put in the extra walls we took out the surplus corridors. The remaining channels of access have all been knocked through.

Vanessa gets off the chair

Vanessa Interconnected?

Cherry Entirely.

Vanessa I must see them at once!
Cherry You said you were going to hang yourself. Have you no sense of commitment?
Vanessa Heaven can wait!
Cherry All right, then — I'll wait with it.

Vanessa exits through door X. Cherry follows

Mother Enid enters through door Y

She is dressed in a long, black habit and white, elaborately constructed head gear. She has pale peach foundation and orange lipstick. She carries a rhinestone-studded cowgirl suit on a hanger. She also carries a guitar, a ten-gallon hat and a bright blonde, ludicrously curly wig. She looks about the room anxiously. She makes for door X, opens it and yelps. She slams the door closed. She makes for door Y, opens it and yelps. She slams it closed. She looks about the room

Seeing the storeroom, she dives into it, pulling the door shut behind her

Cherry enters through door X

She dashes to the trolley and takes her book out from under the cloth. She looks about the room and draws back the shower curtains, then thinks the better of it and swiftly draws them closed again. She makes for door Y, opens it and yelps. She slams the door closed. She thinks for a second, then dashes to the storeroom and tries to open the door. It won't open. She makes for door X and opens it

Barbara enters through door Y

Barbara Cherry! (*She slams door Y behind her*)
Cherry Barbara! (*She slams door X*) What are you doing here?
Barbara Looking for Austin. The cricket team's in crisis. A fielder's injured his foot. He's had to go to hospital.
Cherry Might Austin be there too? After all, Barbara, you're both of you doctors.
Barbara No, Austin's on holiday. What about you?
Cherry I've a Welsh Weekend at the beginning of December. I don't like the sun and I've always been fond of Llanelli.
Barbara No, what are you doing here? The hall's in use tonight. You can't have other bookings.

Cherry (*hiding the book behind her back*) Oh — no! I haven't! No other bookings at all!

Barbara Then you should have gone home.

Cherry Yes, I should. And I did!

Barbara Then why are you back?

Cherry Yes — why am I back? Oh — I heard about the foot! I've come to lend a hand.

Barbara But Austin's the substitute.

Cherry Oh, is he? Right! I'll find him. (*She makes for door X*)

Barbara Just a minute, Cherry. *How* did you hear?

Cherry What?

Barbara About the fielder's foot?

Cherry Erm ... I saw him going to hospital!

Barbara But he's only just left.

Cherry That's right.

Barbara In an ambulance.

Cherry Oh, is that what it was? I thought it looked big for a bandage. (*She continues to head to door X*)

Barbara Where are you going?

Cherry To hide this book! I meant, to look for Austin! (*She pulls open door X*)

Austin Zetanusi enters through door X. He carries a sports bag and a large tin foil parcel

Austin Don't panic! I'm here!

Barbara Austin!

Cherry Oh, good! I'm off ...

Barbara Wait a moment, Cherry. Did you see a nun?

Austin A nun?

Barbara Yes, a nun. You know — black round the edges, with a white bit in the middle.

Austin How long have you been having these colourful delusions?!

Barbara What?

Austin (*offering Cherry the parcel and the bag*) Hold these a moment.

Cherry I can't. (*She produces her book*) I've got my hands full.

Austin Don't argue! (*He snatches the book from Cherry*) I'm a psychiatrist!

He dumps the parcel on Cherry. Cherry shrieks and drops it, then snatches back the book. Austin stares at Cherry in utter disbelief. Cherry goes to door X and opens it

Cherry I never comply with medical advice!

Cherry exits through door X

Austin She's behaving very oddly.
Barbara It's best to ignore her. Get changed quickly — you're needed at the wicket.

Austin takes some cricket pads from his sports bag and starts to strap them on. Barbara opens the foil parcel, revealing sandwiches. This takes some time as each sandwich is individually wrapped

Austin I'm sorry I was late. I was busy developing.
Barbara But you're a fully-grown shrink. You can't possibly get any bigger.
Austin Developing my photograph.
Barbara Photograph? What photograph?
Austin It's really very strange you should think you saw a nun.
Barbara I *did* see a nun!
Austin But there isn't a convent for miles around.
Barbara There's one up near Chieveley.
Austin I've never seen it.
Barbara It's a very old building. It doesn't get about much. I was there last week. One of the nuns chose to die quite suddenly. The Mother Superior, in actual fact.
Austin Did you have to lay her out?
Barbara She was already in the coffin. I had simply to confirm that she was actually dead, and make a formal note of any distinguishing features.
Austin Had she any?
Barbara Yes. Her eyes were open and she had very pragmatic lips.
Austin Pragmatic?
Barbara Distinctly. I used them to seal up a couple of envelopes. I feel guilty about it now.
Austin Which explains your hallucinations.
Barbara What?
Austin Was she wearing make-up?
Barbara Why?
Austin I'm writing a paper. "Mental States Of The Conspicuously Religious, Immediately Prior To Terminal Death." Her choice of cosmetics could be most revealing.
Barbara A pale peach foundation and some very orange lipstick.
Austin She was clearly quite mad.
Barbara Amazing, Austin! How can you tell?

Austin Nobody in their right mind would be seen dead in peach. Was there a psychiatrist present at her passing?

Barbara I don't think Sister Millichope was formally qualified — but she showed a level of indifference that a professional would have been proud of.

Austin Sister Millichope?

Barbara She nursed the Mother through her terminal days. She also bore witness to the Certificate of Death.

Austin Who was the other signatory?

Barbara There wasn't one.

Austin What?

Barbara The rest of the nuns were excluded from the cell. Sister Millichope saw to that.

Austin She's clearly a woman of considerable authority.

Barbara Yes — but she was helped more than somewhat by the Dobermann pinscher.

Austin Dobermann pinscher? That's a very strange practice.

Barbara It's a very strange order. The discipline's ferocious. Few are admitted and no-one ever escapes. They've very nice grounds. An extremely exotic herb garden. A lovely little lily pond ...

Austin Lily pond?

Barbara Yes, lily pond. But the whole thing's enclosed ——

Austin By an electrified fence.

Barbara By an electrified ... What?

Austin The extremely exotic herb garden suddenly joggled my memory. The lovely little lily pond confirmed my recollection. Yes, I've certainly been to that convent myself.

Barbara But you can't become a nun! You're a man.

Austin I'm an atheist. I was up there on a shoot.

Barbara Isn't that rather extreme?

Austin A photographic shoot! I'd been told, by a friend, of some very beautiful newts.

Barbara Some very beautiful what?

Austin Some very beautiful newts.

Barbara But all newts are hideous — it's a well-established fact.

Austin My friend's description suggested quite otherwise. Glorious golden crests — like the sails of a mighty galleon! Glistering, emerald bodies — like the waves of the spangled seas! And that was just the tadpoles. I was determined to capture an adult on film. I set off at once.

Barbara On your photographic shoot of these very beautiful newts?

Austin It was a difficult thing to accomplish.

Barbara It's not that easy to say.

Austin I had little idea of the newt's location — beyond a single supposed sighting somewhere near Chieveley. I searched for what seemed like minutes.

Barbara And did you find them in the end?

Austin No — I found them in the convent.

Barbara Religious Amphibia! Darwin would spin in his grave!

Austin No, not in the building. They were all in the pond.

Barbara But the electrified fence!

Austin I'd taken my telescopic.

Barbara What species are they, exactly? These beautiful newts?

Austin I'm a psychiatrist — not a zoo-keeper!

Barbara Then why did you take the photo?

Austin To enter the competition.

Barbara Competition? What competition?

Austin Your husband's competition.

Barbara Oh, the Appeal Competition! To help win the Appeal.

Austin Yes.

Barbara You needn't have bothered.

Austin What?

Barbara We've lost the Appeal —— (*She breaks off suddenly*)

Austin Pardon?

Barbara Nothing! Give me your photo.

Austin I can't. I haven't got it.

Barbara A disaster in the dark-room? Still, you'd never have won.

Austin Won? Won what?

Barbara Won the competition. It's *way* outside the radius.

Austin Radius? What radius?

Barbara The one around this village. The two-mile radius. It's way, way outside.

Austin What is?

Barbara Chieveley.

Austin I don't understand.

Barbara Didn't you read the rules?

Austin No. I thought it might give me an unfair advantage.

Barbara Rex was trying ——

Austin Was?

Barbara Is! *Is* trying! Rex *is* trying to make the point that we've a vital local wildlife. Unique to this village. Hence — the two-mile rule. All photographs entered must have been taken within it. The radius, I mean. This would have meant — I mean — this *will* mean that Rex can present them to the Ministry as part of the Appeal. It's the whole point of the exercise. To generate some environmental evidence that might have saved—I mean— that might *still* save this village.

Austin Could you run through that again?
Barbara I couldn't even walk it! Look — basically the point is, your picture's redundant.
Austin Useless?
Barbara Absolutely.
Austin Oh. Still — at least I'll get the species identified.
Barbara Pardon?
Austin Rex is an egghead on British Amphibia. And my photo's a peach — if I say so myself.
Barbara But you haven't got the photo.
Austin Of course I haven't. You have.
Barbara What?
Austin I dropped it round to Rex.
Barbara Before you came here?
Austin Forgive me. I was excited. I rang the bell wildly — but there was no reply. I put it through the letter-box. Is Rex all right?

Roger Bloom enters through door X. He is dressed for cricket

Roger Austin! Quickly!
Austin Give me a minute!
Roger Make it sixty seconds!

Roger exits through door X

Austin Now look — about Rex ——
Barbara I've done these sandwiches! Where are the plates?
Austin The plates? They're in my car.
Barbara (*making to exit through door Y*) I'll fetch them at once.
Austin I think I'd better come with you.
Barbara What?
Austin (*producing his car keys*) I've got the keys.
Barbara (*taking them*) Are you stark raving mad?
Austin (*snatching them back*) Don't argue! I'm a psychiatrist!

Barbara and Austin exit through door Y. Barbara takes the sandwiches with her

The storeroom door opens and Enid peers out

She creeps into the room, still carrying the cowgirl suit, etc. She makes for door X

Door X begins to open and Enid darts back into the storeroom

*Cherry enters through door X, carrying the book. She darts to the trolley
and hides it under the cloth. She looks about the room for a moment*

Cherry Where are you!

Vanessa enters through door Y

Vanessa It's amazing! Each room in this hall can be approached not only
swiftly — but without any warning and from *any* direction at all!
Cherry Yet if there's someone you're avoiding you can be certain not to
bump into them. Except, that is, of course, when you're opening a door.
Vanessa It's all most impressive. Was it done for convenience?
Cherry No — just to make things easier. Now — it's time I think, as the
Walrus said, to talk of other things.
Vanessa Of shoes, and ships, and sealing wax? Of cabbages and kings?
Cherry No — I was thinking of strangulation, actually.
Vanessa Oh!
Cherry Didn't you mention suicide? Involving a length of rope? If you'd
like to discuss your worries in confidence, I promise care, compassion and
remarkable understanding.
Vanessa I couldn't!
Cherry Oh, get lost then.
Vanessa All right — you've talked me into it. I live, as I told you, on the new
development.
Cherry Beyond the hill. Not threatened by the bypass.
Vanessa Would that it were!
Cherry What?
Vanessa Threatened, I mean. I don't live there by choice, you see. I'm a
native of this village. I love, adore and cherish every square inch!
Cherry Just a minute!
Vanessa What?
Cherry You were in charge of the nature table!
Vanessa And weren't you the girl having trouble with her mother?
Cherry Vanessa Pile!
Vanessa Cherry Hellingsworth!

They embrace

Cherry Continue your story.

Vanessa On leaving the sixth form I took a job at Telecom. Recruitment. Personnel. I rose quickly through the ranks.

Cherry They recognized your talents and rewarded them accordingly?

Vanessa No — I lied through my teeth and trod all over my friends. I wanted to buy a house — but couldn't afford the village.

Cherry But prices have plummeted. My little house, for instance, has a small but luxurious annexe. Entirely self-contained. One need never see the occupant. I had it built that way on purpose.

Vanessa Why?

Cherry My mother used to live in it. Now, I've been trying to sell that flat for nearly eighteen months. But the property market's dead at the moment. Just like my mother.

Vanessa This was before the threat of the bypass.

Cherry Oh, I see. So what did you do?

Vanessa I bought, like a fool, on the new development. A first-time buyer's package promised the life of Riley. Decorated throughout. Wall to wall ceilings.

Cherry What happened?

Vanessa They went bust. I live now, quite alone, in the middle of a bomb site.

Cherry Would you call it an eyesore?

Vanessa It makes Armageddon look like the Queen Mother's window-box. But that's not the worst. My scheming at BT eventually backfired.

Cherry What?

Vanessa I accidentally sacked myself. Seven hundred and fifty-four!

Cherry Pardon?

Vanessa No — pounds. My mortgage arrears.

Cherry Oh, I see. You mean ... You mean seven hundred and fifty-four pounds?!

Vanessa Exactly. Plus thirty-seven pence.

Cherry Thirty-seven pence?

Vanessa The bus fare to the building society. If I don't pay in cash, by first thing tomorrow, the society in question has promised to pull the plug.

Cherry What?

Vanessa A repossession order.

Cherry No?

Vanessa Yes! I shall lose everything! Oh! What it is to be a female ex-executive, trapped in a hell-hole of negative equity!

Cherry We've all got our problems.

Vanessa What?

Cherry Well — look at me, for instance.

Vanessa A pair of shoddy slingbacks is hardly the end of the world!

Cherry No, not my shoes — my book.

Vanessa Your book?

Cherry My bookings book. I've made a bodge. Oh, it's so embarrassing!

Vanessa An embarrassing book full of bodged-up bookings?

Cherry You've got it.

Vanessa No, I haven't.

Cherry Where is it then? Oh, I remember! (*She fetches the book from the trolley*) Look at that.

Vanessa (*looking at it*) It's an absolute mess.

Cherry Mr Cunningham was impressed by my eagerness to reform. I made no claims to administrative skills.

Vanessa Mr Cunningham?

Cherry Rex. The Chair. The Chair of the committee. He's the person who gave me the job.

Vanessa You mean you get paid for this?!

Cherry No, not at all. My only reward lies in serving this village. I love these people — and they love me. My mother never did — which is why I strangled her. Community Service was a condition of my release. A report on my progress is submitted once a month. Mr Cunningham writes it. My life's in his hands. When he discovers my bodge I'll be banged up forever!

Vanessa What?

Cherry Should my ability to cope ever be called into question, I'll be removed at once and returned to the unit.

Vanessa How would he find out? Mr Cunningham, I mean.

Cherry He'll be down here any minute — to pick up his wife.

Vanessa His wife?

Cherry She's a doctor. First aid for the cricket.

Vanessa But can't you simply hide the book?

Cherry I could — but not the Chickens.

Vanessa What?

Cherry See for yourself.

Vanessa takes the book and looks at it

Vanessa The Southern Fried Chickens?

Cherry Country and Western. A five-piece band.

Vanessa Well, five's not very many. You could surely hide five?

Cherry They've got a new lead singer. Her entourage is enormous.

Vanessa Well, where were you *going* to put them?

Cherry I booked them into the hall.

Vanessa But the hall's already taken.

Cherry Exactly. It's a nightmare! If I had some bullets I'd shoot myself with a gun. If I had a gun.

Vanessa No, I wouldn't do that.

Cherry What?

Vanessa You'd frighten the Hens.

Cherry I don't care about the ... Hens!? What Hens?!

Vanessa The Hens at the Hen night.

Cherry There isn't any Hen night!

Vanessa Oh, yes there is! (*She shows Cherry the book*) *And* a Singing Telegram.

Cherry And a Singing Telegram?! (*She makes for door X*) Where's that rope ... ?

Vanessa (*looking at the book*) Stop!

Cherry Why? Have you found a gun?

Vanessa What are these numbers?

Cherry Numbers?

Vanessa In this book.

Cherry Oh, those. They're my sums.

Vanessa Sums?

Cherry For the Chickens. I placed a couple of ads in the *Newbury Gazette*. I've to pay for the ads from the takings on the door.

Vanessa You mean you're charging for the performance! How much d'you expect to make?

Cherry I'm afraid I don't know.

Vanessa What?

Cherry I didn't arrive at a total. I was multiplying the ads by the takings-away for the Chickens when my attention was divided by the arrival of the Hens.

Vanessa What did they want?

Cherry To leave a deposit.

Vanessa A deposit on what?

Cherry A deposit on their booking.

Vanessa They've paid up front?! Where did you put the cash?

Cherry The strong box in the office.

Vanessa Where did you put the office?

Cherry I left it where it was.

Vanessa makes for door X

Where are you going?

Vanessa Wherever it was that you left it!

Cherry But I don't understand ... Oh, no!

Vanessa Oh, yes!

Cherry Stop! Don't touch that money!

Vanessa Any trouble from you, and I'll squeal to Mr Cunningham!
Cherry You wouldn't? You couldn't!
Vanessa Your optimism's pathetic!

Vanessa exits through door X, slamming it behind her

Cherry Vanessa! Vanessa!

Cherry exits through door X

The storeroom door opens, slowly. Enid peeks out

She creeps into the room, still carrying the cowgirl suit, etc. She makes for door Y. It begins to open

Enid darts back into the storeroom

Garry Alexander enters through door Y. He is dressed for cricket

Garry Austin!

Austin enters through door X

Austin All right!
Garry Well hurry up, will you? It's getting very ugly out there!

Garry exits through door Y

Austin struggles with his cricket pads, which have come unbuckled

Barbara enters through door Y with the sandwiches and some plates

Barbara Austin! Let me help.
Austin No, Barbara. Let *me* help *you*.
Barbara What?

Martin Box enters through door X

Martin Austin!
Austin I'm coming!

Martin exits through door X

Barbara goes to the cupboard and takes out the cricket helmet

Barbara You'll be needing one of these.
Austin Never mind the helmet. It's Rex I'm worried about.
Barbara But ——
Austin Don't argue! I'm a psychiatrist!

Barbara looks at Austin for a moment, then breaks away

Barbara No! (*She moves the trolley to the centre of the room and puts the sandwiches on it. Beaming*) There!
Austin Barbara!
Barbara (*collapsing*) Oh, I feel so guilty spilling the beans! I promised Rex I wouldn't — but ... Oh, I've got to talk to someone!
Austin Very wise, Barbara. Bottling up your beans is a terribly perilous practice. Believe me. I'm a psychiatrist.
Barbara We lost the Appeal. The bypass Appeal.
Austin What!!
Barbara Rex got the letter a fortnight ago.
Austin But why hasn't he broken this calamitous news? The village is on tenterhooks awaiting the decision.
Barbara He's been bottling up his beans.
Austin Ah!
Barbara A practice I know to be terribly perilous.
Austin Who told you that?
Barbara A psychiatrist friend. He's taken it all so personally!
Austin The psychiatrist?
Barbara No — Rex! He has, as you know, been leading the fight. Now that it's lost he thinks it's all his fault.
Austin Well, that's because it is. Has the man no logic?
Barbara He's never liked facing facts. He keeps on hoping for a last minute miracle.
Austin Miracles never happen. It's been proven scientifically. When does the hideous construction work begin?
Barbara First thing in the morning.
Austin What! The village must be told!
Barbara This time tomorrow there won't be any village.
Austin An emergency meeting! Here — in this hall! Tonight!
Barbara I've suggested that already — but Rex won't come.
Austin Agoraphobic depression?
Barbara Possibly, yes. But one thing's for certain.

Austin What?
Barbara He's absolutely shattered and refuses to leave the house.

Steve Marchant enters through door Y

Steve Austin — you're in!
Austin I'll be out straight away.

Steve exits through door Y

Barbara Oh, thank you Austin! Thank you! That you so much! You just
can't imagine how much better I feel!
Austin Of course I can.
Barbara What?
Austin It's easy. I'm a psychiatrist.

Austin exits through door X

*With her back to the storeroom, Barbara arranges the sandwiches on the
plates*

The storeroom door opens. Enid pokes her head out

Barbara makes to put the helmet back in the cupboard

Enid pulls her head back into the storeroom, slamming the door behind her

*Barbara stops and looks at the storeroom door. She puts the helmet in the
cupboard and goes to the storeroom*

*Vanessa dashes in through door Y. She is clutching some bank notes, some
small change and Cherry's book. She slams the door behind her*

*Barbara turns and sees Vanessa but Vanessa doesn't see Barbara as she is
too busy counting the cash. Vanessa moves slowly into the room as she
counts. At the same time Barbara moves slowly towards Vanessa*

Vanessa Seven hundred and fifty-two ... Seven hundred and fifty-three ...
Seven hundred and fifty-four!
Barbara Plus thirty-seven pence.
Vanessa What?
Barbara You've a little loose change in the palm of your hand.
Vanessa Oh ... Thank you. Eeek! Who are you?

Barbara My name is Dr Cunningham.

Vanessa squawks and hides the book and cash behind her back. She dashes to door X

Vanessa Just a minute! (*She opens door X*)
Barbara Stop! Come back!

Vanessa exits through door X, slamming it Barbara's face

Barbara pulls door X open

Enid peeks out of the storeroom

Cherry dashes in through door Y

Cherry Vanessa!

Enid pulls her head back into the storeroom and slams the door shut

Barbara turns. Cherry sees her and squawks. She makes for door Y

Barbara Cherry?
Cherry Barbara!
Barbara What are you doing here? I thought you'd gone home.
Cherry Erm ... (*She snatches up the plates of sandwiches*) These sandwiches!
Barbara What?
Cherry I came back to take them.
Barbara But they're the half-time refreshments. (*She takes the sandwiches back*) And we're not yet semi-complete.
Cherry (*snatching the sandwiches back*) Quite! What? But you were booked into start at ten o'clock this morning!
Barbara No leather struck willow till well after lunch.
Cherry Pardon?
Barbara The other team's minibus got rather behind. Well, no — immediately behind, in actual fact.
Cherry What?
Barbara A hearse, that is.
Cherry A hearse?
Barbara That's right.
Cherry The other team's minibus got stuck behind a hearse?
Barbara It was going to a funeral. Slowly.

Cherry I don't care where it was going, or how fast or otherwise! All I want to know is when you'll be gone.

Barbara Oh, we'll be here all evening.

Cherry What? So Rex won't be down till much, much later? To pick you up, I mean?

Barbara Rex won't be down at the hall at all tonight, Cherry.

Cherry What?

Barbara He's feeling ... well — rather ill.

Cherry Splendid!

Barbara I beg your pardon!?

Vanessa enters through door Y

Vanessa Cherry! (*Seeing Barbara*) Eeek!

Vanessa exits through door Y

Barbara Who was that? She knew your name.

Barbara moves towards door Y. Cherry intercepts her

Cherry I'll do that! You take these!

Cherry thrusts the sandwiches into Barbara's arms and dashes toward door Y. Barbara — bewildered — goes to eat a sandwich. Cherry sees this and walks slowly back to Barbara

Don't pick!

Cherry slaps Barbara's wrist and Barbara drops the sandwich

Cherry dashes out through door Y

Barbara stoops to pick up the sandwich

The storeroom door opens and Enid peeks out. She sees Barbara and withdraws into the storeroom again, slamming the door

Barbara hears the storeroom door slam. Still carrying the sandwiches, she makes toward the storeroom. She pulls at the door, but it won't open

Door Y opens, revealing Vanessa

*She still carries the book and the cash. She looks about the room. She can't
see Barbara since Barbara is at the storeroom door. Vanessa enters the
room, closing the door behind her. Barbara hears Vanessa enter*

Barbara (*turning back into the room*) Eeek!
Vanessa (*seeing Barbara*) Argh!

Vanessa tries to exit. Barbara stops her

Barbara Just a minute! Who are you?
Vanessa You mean you don't remember?

Barbara hands Vanessa the sandwiches and looks her up and down

Barbara Tell me your name.
Vanessa No.
Barbara Why not?
Vanessa I'm insulted you can't remember. (*She moves to door Y, still
  holding the sandwiches, and opens it*) I think you'd better go.
Barbara (*moving to door Y*) I'm sorry it had to end like this.
Vanessa It's better for both of us. Don't forget your tuna and chives. (*She
  gives Barbara the sandwiches*)

  Barbara exits with the sandwiches

Vanessa closes the door and moves towards door X

  Cherry enters through door X

Vanessa squeaks and moves back towards door Y

Cherry (*grabbing her*) Vanessa! You can't go through with this!
Vanessa Oh, yes we can!
Cherry We?! I'm not helping you!
Vanessa I'll squeal to Mr Cunningham!
Cherry You can't! He isn't coming!
Vanessa You're lying! He is!
Cherry I'm not! And he isn't! Besides, it wouldn't be for hours, even if he
  did.
Vanessa Pardon?
Cherry The match was got behind by the minibus's funeral.

Vanessa What?

Cherry Everything's been delayed. Those teams'll be out on that pitch all night.

Vanessa All night?! But that's perfect!

Cherry Bad luck! Pardon?

Vanessa Perfect for our plan!

Cherry Not *our* plan — *your* plan! I'm having nothing to do with it! (*She goes to door Y and opens it*)

Vanessa Cherry?

Cherry (*turning back to Vanessa*) What?

Vanessa Is Rex on the telephone?

Cherry closes door Y and returns to Vanessa

Cherry I knew there'd be a loophole. Oh, why are you doing this to me?!

Vanessa I must have that money!

Cherry No!

Vanessa Look ——— ! (*She hides the book under the trolley*) All we have to do is to get the Chickens in, take the punters' money, and then get them all out again. Simple!

Cherry But where are we going to put them? They're expecting to be in the hall.

Vanessa We'll put them in the Function Suite.

Cherry We haven't got a Function Suite!

Vanessa (*indicating the room*) Oh, yes we have!

Cherry Here?! You must be mad! What about the Cricketers?

Vanessa Exactly! That's the magic!

Cherry What?

Vanessa With everything delayed ——

Cherry They'll all be on the pitch ——

Vanessa Leaving this room clear ——

Cherry For the Southern Fried ——

Vanessa Hen night.

Cherry What?! You can't get the Hens in here as well!

Vanessa I need every penny!

Cherry But you've got their deposit! Isn't that enough?

Vanessa No, not quite.

Cherry What?

Vanessa The bus fare's just gone up.

Cherry But where are we going to put them? The Chickens'll be in here.

Vanessa We'll operate a rota.

Cherry This is madness! Utter madness! Chickens! Hens! Two teams of Cricketers ...

Vanessa But both on the pitch! And Rex isn't coming — so that's you off the hook.

Cherry Off the hook! Off the hook!!

Vanessa You're getting hysterical!

Cherry Of course I'm getting hysterical! Rex might not be coming but what if somebody else turns up? It'll be curtains! Curtains!

Vanessa Pull yourself together! Who else, Cherry, could possibly turn up?

From off, there is the sound of nuns wailing a wretched, dirge-like canticle. Cherry and Vanessa freeze. They look toward door X. Above the wailing, Mother Millichope speaks

Millichope (*off*) This way, Sisters!

Door X opens and Mother Millichope and Sister Tina enter. They are followed by Sister Pybus, Sister Beaverbrook, Sister Howe, Sister Litmus and Sister Small-Change, who are carrying a coffin. Millichope wears a black habit and ornamental head gear (exactly the same as Enid's, in fact). Tina is wearing the plain white habit and wimple of a novice. The other nuns wear black habits and white wimples

The nuns process into the room, carrying the coffin. They stop, solemnly. Millichope turns to Cherry and Vanessa

Millichope Where can we put the Dear Departed?

Zandra Emanuel enters through door Y, dressed for a party

Zandra Is this the place for the Hen night, please?

Cherry screams

Vanessa darts to Zandra and pushes Zandra back out of door Y. She slams the door after her

Vanessa Shut up, Cherry!

Cherry throws her hand over her own mouth

Now then, ladies. How can I help you?

Millichope We've had a major breakdown.

Cherry I know how you feel ——

Vanessa Mental or physical?
Tina Worse than that.
Millichope Mechanical.
Beaverbrook We've experienced problems.
Pybus Just down the road.
Millichope The engine's gone up in flames.
Small-Change The chassis's like a furnace.
Tina And she didn't believe in cremation.
Cherry Who didn't?
Howe Mother Enid.
Litmus So we had to bring her in here.
Vanessa What? Dead? In that coffin?
Cherry But you've got to get her out!
Millichope Impossible, I'm afraid. The lid's screwed down and she's gone
  into rigor mortis. She'll be wedged in that mahogany like a fat girl's foot
  in a pony's stirrup.
Tina If only we had a monkey-wrench.
Millichope Sister Tina! What are you thinking of!
Tina I was only trying to help.
Millichope What help would it be to attack her with a spanner? Dr
  Frankenstein himself could not bludgeon her back into life! We know, dear
  Sister Tina, that you were fond of her more than most — but poor Mother
  Enid's quite dead at the moment. Her spirit has fled. We must allow its
  fleshy receptacle to rest in redundant peace.
Cherry Well, she can't rest in here!
Tina That's what I'm saying.
Millichope What?
Tina If we only had some tools I'm sure I could fix the engine.
Millichope Well, don't look at me! I haven't even a screwdriver! I'm a
  woman at one with God — not Tool-kit Tilly!
Tina Who mentioned screwdriver?
Vanessa We've got some tools — haven't we, Cherry?
Cherry Have we? Oh, yes!

Zandra enters through door Y

Zandra Look — what's going on?
Cherry Eeek!
Vanessa You're going out!

Vanessa dashes to Zandra and pushes her back out through door Y

Vanessa Cherry! The ladies!

Cherry They're occupied at the moment.

Vanessa *These* ladies, Cherry! Lead them to the monkey-wrench! I'll look out the posi-drive and be with you in a minute.

Vanessa exits through door Y

Millichope Sisters — lay down your burden and attend to your task. I shall watch over the bag. I mean — the body!

The nuns deposit the coffin on the trolley. Millichope moves to the coffin and stands over it solemnly

Cherry This way, ladies.

Cherry exits through door Y. All the nuns follow, except Tina

Tina lingers and Millichope glares at her

Tina exits through door Y

Millichope closes door Y after Tina. She takes a very long, pump-action screwdriver from her habit. She goes to the coffin and swiftly unscrews the lid. She lifts the lid a little and looks inside, then replaces it

Tina enters through door X. She carries a very long, pump-action screwdriver

Tina It's no good, Mother Millichope! I must look on her beatitude just one last time!

Millichope (*hiding her own screwdriver under her habit*) Put that away! You've seen her already.

Tina Days ago, alas! Before the Dobermann pinscher.

Millichope (*snatching the screwdriver out of Tina's hands*) No! It would only upset you!

Tina Upset me? I'm in grief already!

Vanessa dashes in through door X

Vanessa Ah! (*She snatches the screwdriver from Millichope*)

Millichope What?

Vanessa And shift that coffin! There's a Policeman coming.

Tina A Policeman?!
Vanessa Just shift it!

Vanessa exits through door Y

Millichope lifts one end of the coffin lid

Millichope Help me, Sister Tina!!
Tina Why?
Millichope I refuse to respond to this searing interrogation!

She drops the coffin lid and it slides off

I am Mother Superior, now! And by Mother Enid's own decree! Remember that, Sister Tina!
Tina How could I forget? It was a most unlikely appointment! You're never in contemplation for being always amongst the exotic herbs!
Millichope If you have any queries regarding my shrubs I suggest that you address them to Mother Superior Enid! She, I can assure you, approved of my cultivations!
Tina But Mother Enid's dead! I can't address her at all!
Millichope Are you doubting the power of prayer?! Tina, my dear — you've been at the convent such a very short time. Can we be sure of the sincerity of your calling?
Tina You wouldn't give me the elbow?
Millichope You're forcing my hand!
Tina But entry into the order has always been my dream! I'd give up just about everything to be a fully-fledged nun!
Millichope Of course you would, you idiot! That's all part of the deal!
Tina My heart is astonished, beyond all corporal measure, by your penetrating insight and firm, invaluable guidance. I trust you, rather suddenly. I'll do anything you say.
Millichope Help me with this coffin.

She picks up the lid and hands it to Tina, then produces her own screwdriver

Tina Where did you get that?
Millichope I never travel without my screwdriver. One should always have something sensational to do in the train. Put on the lid.
Tina And then put on the lid!
Millichope What?
Tina Shakespeare.
Millichope Never heard of him. Quickly, Tina, quickly!

Tina goes to the coffin and looks inside. She screeches and drops the lid

Millichope Sister Tina!
Tina Mother Millichope ...

She lifts, from the coffin, a large black bin-bag

What have you done?!!
Millichope Don't panic, don't panic! It's only a bag of mud.
Tina Mud?
Millichope Yes, mud! (*She snatches the bag from Tina and puts it back in the coffin*)
Tina But where's Mother Enid!
Millichope I'm afraid I've no idea.
Tina What?
Millichope Can you listen very quickly?
Tina Why?
Millichope I've to speak extremely fast. There's a Policeman coming.
Tina Oh! The Policeman!

Tina makes to exit. Millichope grabs her

Millichope Lie on the floor.
Tina Why? Is he armed?
Millichope The story I'm to tell you is absolutely horrific. The air up here is thin. Should you go into shock you'll find it difficult to breathe.
Tina Before I was initiated I'd often wear high-heels. My lungs are accustomed to altitude. You can tell me the absolute worst.

Pause

Millichope Mother Enid was unholy.
Tina No!
Millichope Yes! She longed for Dolly Parton.
Tina What!
Millichope The music of, I mean. Did you ever look in her Walkman? Not, as she always claimed, the comforts of Handel — but "Dolly's All Time Hits"; "Way Down Deep With Dolly". Why she took orders in the first place, I'm afraid we'll never know. Her rise to Mother Superiorhood is a mystery which passeth any understanding. But I tell you this, Sister Tina, Mother Enid was desperate! Desperate to escape! She knew me to be a dab

hand in the herb department. She suggested a wheeze. I should concoct a somnambulizing draught which, when imbibed, produced all the symptoms of apparent death. This, to me, was easy. I have a library of such recipes endorsed by Barbara Cartland. The effect was remarkable. It convinced, quite entirely, a reputable medic. Post her supposed death, Mother Enid fled the convent — leaving her mantle. Or should I say her habit? No — I shouldn't. I had to have a new one made. Hers didn't fit me ...

Tina What?

Millichope The point is, Tina — I took over the reins. This was my "payoff". I hope you understand?

Tina I understand entirely.

Millichope Good.

Tina But don't believe a word of it!

Millichope Tina!

Tina Mother Superior Enid was the personification of Goodness!

Millichope No!

Tina Yes!

Millichope Listen! Remember you assured me I could tell you the absolute worst?

Tina Did I?

Millichope Well, I'm going to. When you first arrived at the convent, you were a ghastly bottle blonde. Fluorescent canary with corkscrew curls. These were, of course, shorn off at initiation.

Tina My heart leaps up at the memory! It was my proudest moment! They were taken away by Oxfam to be made into universal plumbing joints for the somewhat over-privileged of the village.

Millichope No, Sister Tina — I'm afraid they were not!

Tina What!

Millichope The day your superfluous ringlets were due to be despatched I caught Mother Enid sitting bolt upright in her pretended sick-bed. She was working at her tapestry loom.

Tina Tapestry cleanses the soul. She told me so herself.

Millichope She wasn't making a tapestry.

Tina What?

Millichope No! She was making a wig.

Tina A wig?!

Millichope Yes, a wig! Out of *your* hair!

Tina Oh! (*She goes into a wild fit; spluttering, gasping, gagging for breath. She eventually regains control*)

Millichope Well?

Tina I've made a radical reassessment of Mother Enid's character. I see her, now, to be the embodiment of sin. I cannot, however, approve of your wheeze. You should have done her in entirely, or else not bothered at all. Inducing semi-death is not only a waste of time but is also, almost certainly, in very poor taste. When the Policeman arrives I shall have to tell him everything.

Millichope But you can't, Sister Tina! They'll think me a murderess!

Tina You need only produce Sister Enid in order to clear your name.

Millichope I can't produce Sister Enid! I don't know where she is!

Tina Hard Cheddar cheese. I must tell the truth. It was one of my vows.

Millichope But you're a novice, you absolute idiot! You haven't yet taken your vows!

Tina I've been practising, haven't I?!

Millichope And that's all you'll ever do!

Tina What?

Millichope Practise! Unless you promise, Sister Tina, to keep your mouth *shut* I shall see to it, I warn you, that you never become a nun!

Tina I won't take orders from you, Mother Millichope!

Millichope That's exactly my point! I shall deny you entry into the Order — forever!

Pause. The two women stare at each other. Tina darts to the coffin and tries to lift it, but can't

Tina It won't budge an inch!

Millichope It's on a trolley — fool!

They push the trolley (with the coffin on it) backwards into the shower. When they get into the shower the coffin slips off the trolley so that it is protruding into the room slightly and facing the audience on an angle. Millichope notices that the lid is still on the floor in the room

Tina! The lid!

Tina darts to the lid. Millichope pulls the shower curtains closed so that she is now inside the shower, behind the curtains. The coffin protrudes from the curtains slightly

Zandra enters through door Y. Vanessa follows

Zandra Right — where can we put my Policeman?

Tina Policeman! Argh!

Tina thrusts the coffin lid at Zandra. Zandra grabs it, bewildered

Zandra What?

Vanessa grabs the lid from Zandra

Tina runs out through door Y

Vanessa Thank you — I was looking for this!
Zandra What on earth is it?
Vanessa Oh, it's nothing on earth.
Zandra What?
Vanessa No. It's made for the water! A surfboard, you see?
Zandra But there isn't any water.
Vanessa Yes, there is! Outside!

Vanessa thrusts Zandra out through door Y

*Vanessa turns into the room and stands with the lid in front of her so that
Millichope, who comes out of the shower, cannot see her properly*

Millichope Sister Tina? (*She moves toward Vanessa*) Sister Tina!

She pulls at the coffin lid and reveals Vanessa

Argh!

Millichope darts out through door Y, leaving her screwdriver behind

Vanessa Just a minute!

*But Millichope has gone. Vanessa looks at the lid for a moment, not knowing
what to do with it. She pulls back the shower curtain, tosses the lid into the
shower — she doesn't really take in the coffin — and closes the curtains*

(*Making for door X*) Zandra! (*She stops dead and looks back towards the
shower, horrified. She moves towards it*)

Zandra enters through door Y

Zandra I couldn't see any water ——
Vanessa (*turning back to Zandra*) Argh!
Zandra What's in there?

Zandra makes for the shower. Vanessa grabs her and pulls her away

Vanessa Nothing! Just a dead nun! I mean — dead fun!

Zandra What?

Vanessa Surfing! Isn't it? Dead fun. Ny. Fun-ny. When you fall off. Ha ha ha!

Zandra Have you gone mad?

Vanessa No, not yet — but it's a very appealing option. Where's your Telegram?

Zandra Out in the car.

Vanessa We must fetch him at once!

Vanessa opens door Y

Zandra exits through door Y

Vanessa slams the door after her

The storeroom door opens and Enid pokes her head out

Vanessa makes for the shower

Enid withdraws swiftly into the storeroom again

Cherry enters through door Y and freezes in the doorway

Cherry Argh!

Vanessa turns

Cherry Where's the coffin?!

Vanessa Er ... they've taken it away!

Cherry Thank goodness! (*She slams the door closed behind her*)

Vanessa What?

Cherry I was brought up by nuns. Such things leave their mark. The presence of a Sister simply cripples me with guilt.

Vanessa Even a dead one?

Cherry Especially a dead one! I couldn't possibly go through with this plan if that corpse was still in this hall!

Vanessa Couldn't you?

Cherry Not a hope.

Vanessa Well, it's gone.

Cherry Are you sure?

Vanessa Yes — positive! Where will I find some cushions?

Cherry Cushions?

Vanessa Yes — cushions! You can't have a function suite with hard bottomed chairs!

Cherry But this isn't a function suite!

Vanessa That's why I need the cushions!

Cherry The fold-up bed.

Vanessa What?

Cherry Under it, I mean.

Vanessa Excellent! Excellent! I'll get the coffin — I mean, cushions!

Cherry Pardon?

Vanessa You deal with the Policeman.

Cherry Policeman? What Policeman? Oh! Mr Cunningham!

Vanessa What?

Cherry He's told the Bill about my bodge!

Vanessa How could he have, Cherry?! He isn't even here! And it's not a *real* policeman!

Cherry What?

Vanessa No! It's the Singing Telegram.

Cherry Oh, the Singing ——

Vanessa Yes! For the Hen night. Now get out there and sort it.

Vanessa thrusts Cherry out through door Y

Vanessa slams the door after her

Enid peeks out of the storeroom

Vanessa gingerly makes for the shower

Enid swiftly withdraws into the storeroom

Vanessa, at the shower, toys with the curtains. She pulls herself together and takes a deep breath as:

Rex enters through door X, carrying a photograph of a newt. He is extremely excited

Rex Cherry!

Vanessa Argh! (*She pulls away from the shower*)

Rex Oh, I'm terribly sorry. I thought you were Miss Hellingsworth. You haven't seen my wife, have you?

Vanessa Who?

Rex Barbara.

Vanessa (*horrified*) Mrs Cunningham!

Rex Yes.

Vanessa Oh, no ——

Rex But ——

Vanessa What are you doing here!?

Rex Looking for ——

Vanessa Cherry? I mean — Miss Hellingsworth! Well, I'm sorry Rex — I'm afraid she's gone home.

Rex What?

Vanessa She had no other bookings, you see. No other bookings at all tonight!

Rex No, not Cherry. I'm looking for Austin.

Vanessa Who?

Rex He left me this photogra —— Just a minute. Who are you?

Vanessa Me? Oh ... I'm the cabbie!

Rex The cabbie?

Vanessa Yes, that's right! I've come to pick up Cherry! I mean — Miss Hellingsworth!

Rex But you said she'd gone home.

Vanessa Has she? Right. Then so must I.

Rex What?

Vanessa Go. Goodbye!

Vanessa makes for door Y. Rex makes for door X. Vanessa opens door Y

Cherry starts to enter through door Y. She is leading Keith Lumpley. Keith is dressed in a brightly patterned shell suit. He carries a sports bag. Zandra follows

Cherry Vanessa — this is the Tele ——

Vanessa shrieks. Rex turns back into the room

Vanessa slams the door on Cherry, Keith and Zandra, and it hits Keith in the face

Keith yells from behind the door

Rex Why did you shriek?
Vanessa Er ... I saw your wife!

There is a groan from Keith behind the door

Rex (*making for door Y*) She sounds like she's in pain!

Vanessa stops Rex and turns him around. She drags him to door X

Vanessa No, she sounds like she's out here!

Rex exits through door X

Vanessa slams the door after him. She stands with her back against the door for a moment. She glances at the shower and gingerly moves towards it. She goes to open the curtains

Barbara enters through door Y. She is still carrying her sandwiches

Barbara Cherry!
Vanessa Argh! (*She pulls away from the shower*)
Barbara Oh, I'm terribly sorry. I thought you were Miss Hellingsworth. You haven't seen my husband, have you?
Vanessa You said Cherry! I mean — Miss Hellingsworth!
Barbara No, Cherry's gone home. But my husband's just arrived.
Vanessa Has he? I haven't seen him! (*She makes for door X*)
Barbara Just a minute! Who are *you*?
Vanessa Very good question. I'll go and find out.

Vanessa goes to door Y and opens it

Cherry attempts to come in with Keith and Zandra

Cherry Vanessa ——
Vanessa No!

She slams the door on them, hitting Keith in the face

Barbara What was that?
Vanessa What was what?

There is a groan from Keith behind the door

Barbara (*making for door Y*) That!
Vanessa (*apprehending Barbara*) Oh, that! Quickly! Out there! (*She points at door Y*)
Barbara What?
Vanessa It might be rather dangerous!
Barbara Dangerous?
Vanessa Rather.

There is a loud groan from Keith

Quickly! Quickly!

Vanessa drags Barbara to door X and thrusts her out, slamming the door after her

Now — cushions! No, coffin! No! The Singing Policeman! (*She goes to door Y and opens it*) Cherry!

But Cherry, Zandra and Keith have gone

Cherry ... ?

Vanessa exits through door Y

Cherry enters through door X. Zandra, who is supporting Keith, stands in the doorway behind her

Cherry Right, quickly! Get him in.

Zandra and Keith attempt to come in to the room

Rex enters through door Y

Rex Austin?
Cherry Eeek!

Cherry slams door X on Zandra and Keith, hitting Keith on the head

Rex Cherry!
Cherry Mr Cunningham!

There is a groan from Keith behind the door

Rex Pardon?

Cherry lets out a screech in order to cover Keith's groan

What?

Cherry I caught my cushions! I mean — I caught my fingers! (*She makes for door X*)

Rex Fingers? An accident? (*Calling off*) Barbara! First aid!

Cherry No! No! Please!

Rex Who was that man? Oh! Was it the Inspector?!

Cherry Inspector!? You've called the Police! (*She falls to her knees, begging*) Oh, please Mr Cunningham! Let me explain!

Rex There's no time for that!

Rex makes for door X. Cherry grabs him around the legs

Cherry But it's not the Inspector!

Rex It's not? Then who is it?

Barbara enters through door Y, carrying the sandwiches

Barbara Rex?!

Rex Oh, don't be silly, Barbara — I'd have recognized Rex!

Cherry (*releasing Rex*) Ooh! Mr Cunningham!

Rex (*making for door Y*) I shall investigate!

Barbara Where are you going?!

Rex throws door Y open

Vanessa enters through door Y. She carries a huge pile of cushions, table-cloths etc., that partly obscure her face

Vanessa (*staggering forward*) I found the cushions!

Cherry (*burying her face in her hands*) Oh, no! Oh, no ——

Vanessa Eeek! Mr Cunningham!

Vanessa screams and hurls the remaining cushions over her head. They hit Barbara in the face. Barbara recoils with a moan

Vanessa thrusts Rex out through door X. Rex screams

Rex (*as he is being pushed out*) Barbara!

Vanessa slams the door on Rex

Barbara Out of my way — whoever you are! (*She pushes Vanessa aside and opens door X*) Rex!

Rex attempts to come in, waving his photograph

Rex Barbara!
Barbara (*turning back to Vanessa*) Just a minute!

Barbara slams the door closed, hitting Rex in the face

Who *are* you, exactly?

There is a groan from Rex, off

Rex, my dearest darling!

She opens door X. There is nobody there

Vanessa (*turning swiftly to Cherry*) Who am I, exactly?
Cherry A friend of Austin's!
Vanessa Austin? Who's Austin?
Cherry Don't argue! You're a psychiatrist!

We hear Rex's voice from somewhere beyond door Y

Rex (*off*) Austin?! Inspector?!
Barbara (*turning back into the room distractedly*) My husband!
Cherry Over here!

Cherry goes to door Y. Vanessa slams door X shut. Cherry opens door Y

Zandra attempts to come in, supporting Keith

Zandra Thank you! Can you take him?
Cherry No!

Cherry thrusts Zandra and Keith back out through door Y. She slams the door, hitting Keith on the head

Barbara Who was that?
Vanessa Who was what?

There is a groan from Keith behind the door

Barbara It sounds like my husband!
Cherry I shall investigate!

Cherry darts through door Y. Barbara gives chase

   Cherry slams the door in Barbara's face

Barbara pulls at the handle

Barbara Oh, really ...

Barbara marches to door X, and finds Vanessa standing in front of it

   Out of my way!

Vanessa moves

   Barbara exits through door X. She slams it behind her

Vanessa moves to door Y and opens it

Vanessa Cherry!

   Barbara enters through door X

Barbara Just a minute!
Vanessa (*turning*) What? (*She slams door Y*)
Barbara Have you decided who you are?
Vanessa Yes. I'm a friend of Austin's.
Barbara I've never seen you with him.
Vanessa Don't argue! I'm a psychiatrist!

Vanessa opens door Y and makes to exit

Barbara Really?! Thank goodness! (*She slams door X and moves to Vanessa*)

Vanessa What?! (*She slams door Y and moves to Barbara*)
Barbara My husband's agoraphobic. Or I should say he *was*.
Vanessa Pardon?
Barbara I take it you're fully qualified?
Vanessa I bring my own cushions.
Barbara Oh, what a comfort! Please help me, Doctor. I need expert advice.
Vanessa (*appalled*) Expert?! Advice?!
Barbara Yes.
Vanessa If you get it will you go?
Barbara As soon as I've got an answer.
Vanessa An answer? To what?
Barbara Only this morning he was a textbook case.
Vanessa How do you know?
Barbara I looked in the textbook.
Vanessa What?

Barbara hands the sandwiches to Vanessa and takes a book from her pocket

(*Handing the sandwiches back to Barbara*) I must have that at once!
Barbara Why?
Vanessa (*taking the book*) I want to press a flower.
Barbara My trust in you, Doctor, grows by the second!
Vanessa (*glancing, stealthily, at the book*) A textbook case you say?
Barbara Agoraphobic. Yes.
Vanessa Shattered? Withdrawn? Refusing to leave the house?
Barbara Quite. Yet mere hours later he's here in this hall — running around like a baby and calling out for Austin. I wonder — perhaps — has he finally gone quite mad?
Vanessa There's no doubt about it.
Barbara Are you certain?
Vanessa Quite.

Vanessa closes the book and offers it to Barbara

Now go.
Barbara But I can't! Not yet! You must explain his condition!
Vanessa Explain? His condition? (*Glancing at the book*) Erm ... Ah! Violent mood swings.
Barbara Violent? Is he dangerous?
Vanessa Only to himself.
Barbara But I don't ... Oh! He wouldn't!
Vanessa I'm sorry — but he might. At the moment he's euphoric ...
Barbara Euphoric? What does that mean?

Vanessa (*glancing at the book*) Erm ... Entirely possessed by a sense of great joy. Most abnormal. Should he get a nasty shock then he'll almost certainly topple. I mean top. Himself.

Barbara Top himself?

Vanessa Suicide!

Barbara Oh! What sort of a shock?

Vanessa Well ... Erm ... A piece of bad news, for instance, regarding the bypass.

Barbara He's had the bad news regarding the bypass.

Vanessa Well, if he gets any more be sure not to give it to him.

Barbara What?

Vanessa The consequences, I warn you, could be absolutely dire.

Barbara Dire?

Vanessa Yes — *dire*! And now you must go ——

Barbara Will there be any danger signs? If he's getting near the edge, I mean.

Vanessa (*glancing at the book*) Er ... They sometimes hear voices.

Barbara Voices?

Vanessa Only sometimes.

Barbara I'll bear that in mind. Voices. Very well. Goodbye, Doctor. I've sandwiches to see to.

Vanessa Don't forget your book.

Barbara hands Vanessa the sandwiches and takes the book

Barbara I can see you're very honest. My trust in you is total. I shall certainly recommend you to my more neurotic friends.

Vanessa opens door X for Barbara

Vanessa Why, by the way, do you carry it with you?

Barbara The sandwiches?

Vanessa No, the book.

Barbara Oh — to ward off bogus psychiatrists. There are so many of them about!

Barbara exits through door X

Vanessa Now — what next? (*She realizes she is holding the sandwiches, and puts them down. She makes for door X and opens it*) Cherry! Cherry!

There is a groan from Enid in the storeroom. Vanessa freezes. She slams door

Y and looks at the shower. She creeps toward it gingerly. She puts her hand on the curtains

Door Y opens and Cherry dashes in

Cherry Vanessa!
Vanessa (*spinning round*) Argh!
Cherry I've lost the Singing Telegram!
Vanessa What? And Zandra? Out of my way!

Vanessa dashes for door Y. Cherry follows

Cherry Vanessa!

Vanessa and Cherry exit through door Y

The room is quite empty for a moment

The storeroom door opens and Enid pokes her head out. She wears a ten-gallon hat, with a wig on top of it. She is wearing her cowgirl outfit, with the guitar over her shoulder. She looks about the room and creeps out. She makes for door X and opens it

Barbara enters through door X

Barbara Have you seen my tuna and chives?

Enid squeals and turns away

I can't leave without them. I'm sure I left them here ...

Enid moves towards the sandwiches, all the while keeping her back to Barbara. She picks up sandwiches and hands them to Barbara, without turning to face her. Barbara is bewildered

Oh, thank you.

Barbara goes to exit through door X. She stops and looks back at Enid, who is still standing with her back to her

Barbara pauses, shakes her head and exits through door X

Enid dashes to door Y

Cherry opens door Y and attempts to come in. Zandra, supporting Keith, follows

Enid shrieks and slams the door on them, hitting Keith in the face

There is a yell from Keith on the other side of the door. Enid makes for door X. She is about to about to open it when she notices her reflection in the mirror. She sees that her wig is on top of the hat. She hastily switches the hat and wig and turns back to check herself in the mirror. She makes to open door X. There is a groan from Keith outside and Enid recoils. She makes for door Y

Door Y opens suddenly and Enid recoils

The other Southern Fried Chickens tumble in (Lolita Fenetre, Blanche July, Aramist Sweet-Bird II and Cyd Spank). None of them are in their stage costumes, but each of them carries a tiny valise. They are squawking in unison

Chickens Tallulah!
Enid Girls! What are you doing here?
Lolita Honey — we simply couldn't sit out in that parking lot one iddy minute longer!
Cyd We must have refreshment!
Aramist If we're to sing at all!
Blanche My throat's as poached as a bullfrog's in August!
Lolita Why you kept us there in the first place, I simply can't imagine.
Enid I had to check.
Chickens Check? Check what?
Enid The acoustics. And they're terrible.
Lolita (*singing*) "Stand by your man!"
Cyd Beautiful, Lolita.
Blanche Sounds fine to me.
Cyd Exactly, Blanche.
Aramist Nothing wrong here.
Cyd I'm with you, Aramist.
Lolita Will you shut up, Cyd!
Enid The point is, you see — this isn't the hall.
Aramist Isn't the hall?
Enid No. It's ... the laundry!

Blanche The laundry!?
Enid Yes!
Aramist (*to Lolita*) You booked us into a wash-room?!
Lolita I did no such thing! (*To Enid*) What's going on here?!
Enid Not us for a start.
Lolita I beg your pardon?
Cyd Beg away, Lolita! Give her what for!
Aramist But we've got to perform!
Cyd Aramist is right!
Blanche We need the green stuff!
Cyd Sure thing, Blanche!
Lolita Will you shut up, Cyd! Tallulah, honey — are you saying you've
    cancelled the show?
Enid No. Not yet.
Blanche Not yet?!
Aramist Not never!
Lolita Now, let's get this straight. We four girls have been together fifteen
    years.
Blanche Sixteen.
Aramist Counting Memphis.
Cyd And the weekend in Dagenham.
Lolita
Aramist } (*together*) Shut up, Cyd!
Blanche
Lolita Whereas you, Tallulah Honey, only joined this band last week.
Aramist You didn't even provide your own costume!
Enid I provided the wig!
Aramist How she could dream of turning up at the audition in those hideous
    black rags, I never will know!
Blanche She still runs around in them. For day-wear, I mean.
Aramist What are they — antique?
Blanche I've never seen anything like it!
Cyd I have!
Aramist } (*together*) What?
Blanche
Cyd In *The Sound of Mus* ——
Lolita Cyd! Shut up! But you had a pretty neat voice.
Blanche So we took you on.
Aramist Provided your outfit.
Blanche Even your guitar.
Lolita And why was that, Tallulah? 'Cause we thought you were one of us!
Blanche A trooper!

Aramist Not a whiner!
Enid But surely I'm allowed my say?
Aramist What are you implying?
Blanche The Southern Fried Chickens are democratic to the bone!
Lolita Sure!
Cyd That's right!
Lolita *I* make all the decisions! And if you don't like it, honey — there's the door!
Enid Are you saying I'm out? But I'd die if you dump me!
Lolita Well, that's the deal. You either stay here, and sing — or leave the band, and croak!

Pause

Enid There isn't any option.
Blanche What?
Enid I'm afraid I've got to croak.

She hands the guitar to Lolita

Here.
Aramist Where are you going?
Enid There. (*She makes for door X*)
Cyd Stop her, Lolita! We're nothing without her voice!

Enid opens door X

> *Cherry tries to come in with Keith, who is supported by Zandra and Vanessa*

Cherry Put him over ——

Cherry sees Enid. Enid shrieks

> *Enid slams the door on them, hitting Keith in the face*

Keith yells, behind the door

Lolita What was that?
Enid Me. Croaking.
Lolita Lordy!

There is a groan from Keith behind the door

Enid Oh! There I go again.
Lolita You wouldn't *really* leave us — would you, Tallulah honey?
Enid (*taking back the guitar*) Of course I wouldn't. Would you like to dress?
Cyd Where?
Enid In the dressing-room.
Aramist Oh, we do have a dressing-room?
Enid Of course. Over here.

Enid goes to the storeroom and opens the door

  The Chickens squawk with delight and pile into the room

*Enid slams the door on them. As she does this the squawking stops
immediately (this establishes that the room is sound-proof). Enid goes to lock
the door. She discovers there is no key. She looks about the room and sees the
cupboard. She drags it in front of the storeroom door, with the door of the
cupboard facing out into the room. She collapses — exhausted — against the
cupboard. She makes for door X, opens it and squeals. She closes door X and
dives into the cupboard*

  Barbara and Austin enter from door X. Barbara has the sandwiches

Barbara Look!
Austin Where?
Barbara But ... (*She looks about, bewildered*) She was here just a minute
  ago.
Austin In a ten-gallon hat?
Barbara Yes.
Austin Another hallucination?
Barbara You think I'm going mad? Oh! Have I got it from Rex?
Austin Rex? What are you talking about?
Barbara I'm talking about your friend!
Austin Of course Rex is my friend ——
Barbara What?
Austin But I can't discuss him now.
Barbara Pardon?
Austin I'm needed at the wicket, Barbara! (*He makes for door X*)
Barbara Austin! Please! You *have* to wear a helmet! (*She puts down the
  sandwiches and goes to where the cupboard used to be*) Eeek!
Austin Pardon?

Barbara Now the cupboard's disappeared!
Austin What!
Barbara Oh, no! It's over here.

She goes to the cupboard and opens the door, revealing Enid. Enid hands her the helmet

Barbara Thank you. (*She closes the cupboard door*)

Ian Blane enters from door Y

Ian Come on, Austin!
Austin I'm coming! I'm coming!

Ian exits through door Y. Austin exits as well, slamming the door after him

Barbara puts down the helmet and dashes to door Y

Barbara Austin! (*She pulls open the door*) Your helmet! (*She realizes she hasn't got it, slams the door and picks up the helmet. She moves back to door Y*)

Enid comes out of the cupboard and moves to door X. She sees Barbara and freezes. Barbara opens door Y, stops and turns back. Enid picks up the sandwiches and hands them to Barbara

(*Moving forward to collect them*) Oh, thank you so much. I knew I'd left them somewhere.

Barbara moves back to door Y. Enid darts to door X and opens it. Barbara suddenly shrieks, tossing the sandwiches into the air. She turns back to Enid

Stop! Where did you come from?
Enid (*keeping her back to Barbara*) I'm after Miss Hellingsworth. Am I before her?
Barbara What?
Enid Are you she?
Barbara Me?
Enid Yes.
Barbara No. Cherry isn't here. Who are you?
Enid Right. Good. Then neither am I.
Barbara What?

Enid Here! Me! I'm not! And never have been! Goodbye!!

Enid makes to exit

Barbara Wait!

Enid freezes

Enid What?

Barbara goes to Enid and pulls her around, so they are face to face

Barbara I asked you who you were.
Enid (*pulling at her wig in an effort to hide her face*) Yes! And still I am!
Barbara Who?
Enid You mean — you don't know?
Barbara Should I?
Enid I hope not. Are you saying you don't recognize me?
Barbara Yes.
Enid No idea who I am?
Barbara No.
Enid Definitely?
Barbara Positively.
Enid My name is Tallulah! Of The Southern Fried Chickens! Miss Hellingsworth's expecting us.
Barbara Oh. To perform?
Enid In the hall. Only we can't.
Barbara Why not?
Enid Because you're here. I mean — the floor here.
Barbara What?
Enid The floor here. Floor. Here. Bad acoustics. Terrible. Can't be done.
Barbara It couldn't be anyway.
Enid Couldn't be anyway what?
Barbara Couldn't be anyway done. At least not tonight. There's a play in the hall. Amateur dramatics.
Enid A terrible mistake!
Barbara That's what I said — but they managed to sell the tickets.
Enid I mean there's *been* a mistake. On the part of Miss Hellingsworth. I must speak to her at once! When she comes back can you tell her I've gone?
Barbara Certainly. What? But you've only just arrived.
Enid I shouldn't like to outstay my welcome. (*She makes to exit*)
Barbara You've very good habits.
Enid What?

Barbara Habits.
Enid Habits?!
Barbara Socially speaking. Yours are very good.
Enid Oh, I see. Yes. Thank you. I always try my best. (*She makes to exit*)
Barbara Some people have none.
Enid Nun?!
Barbara Habits.
Enid Nuns! Habits! What are you suggesting?
Barbara Nothing.
Enid Good.
Barbara Good?
Enid Yes. Good. Bye. Goodbye. I'm going.
Barbara Oh, you're going?
Enid Yes. Ta-ta! (*She makes to exit*)
Barbara Just a minute.
Enid What?
Barbara Why are you wearing that hideous wig?
Enid How dare you?
Barbara I'm a doctor.
Enid You think I don't know that?! (*She makes to exit through door Y*)
Barbara Just a minute.
Enid (*turning back to Barbara*) What?!
Barbara Is that a pale peach pancake? And you've very pragmatic lips ...
Enid Pragmatic?
Barbara Distinctly. Where are you from?
Enid Way down deep. Texas, to be exact.
Barbara Is that anywhere near Chieveley?
Enid No — another continent!
Barbara Are you sure that's not a wig?
Enid Yes.
Barbara A piece?
Enid No.
Barbara Extensions possibly?
Enid Nothing!
Barbara All right! Keep your hair on ...

Enid's hands fly to her wig

Darren Spavin enters through door X. He's dressed for cricket

Darren Barbara — quickly!
Barbara Oh! Have you found Rex?!

Darren It's Austin *I'm* worried about!
Barbara Austin? An accident!
Darren No — but there will be!
Barbara What?
Darren Their bowler's ferocious! And Austin's in bat!
Barbara Oh! Give him this helmet!

Barbara hands the helmet to Darren

Darren He refuses to wear it!
Barbara Out of my way! (*She moves to door X*)
Darren Who are you?
Enid My name is Tallulah!
Barbara Of The Southern Fried Chickens!

Barbara exits through door X

Darren Oh.

Darren goes to Enid, shakes her hand, and draws her toward him

  Spice to meet you.

Darren stares at Enid's wig and continues to clasp her hand. Enid smiles broadly. She peels Darren's fingers away from her hand and shuffles backwards slightly. Darren pursues her stealthily

Enid She's forgotten the helmet. And the tuna and chives.
Darren What? Oh ... thank you.

Darren picks up the empty plate and puts it under his arm. He makes to exit through door X. He takes his spectacles from his pocket and puts them on. He peers at Enid. Enid turns and sees Darren staring at her. She smiles broadly

  If she asks about the tuna and chives — I've put them in the kitchen. OK?

Enid nods elegantly. Her wig slips. She recovers as best she can. Darren waves. Enid waves back regally

  Darren exits through door X

Enid slams the door after him and collapses with a sigh. She takes off her hat and wig and fans herself with the hat. She makes for door Y

Door Y opens. Darren puts his head in

Darren (*indicating her wig with the helmet*) I say?

Enid squeaks. She snatches the helmet out of Darren's hands and turns away. She pulls on the helmet, throwing the hat on top of the helmet and the wig on top of the hat

Enid (*grandly*) Yes?
Darren Is that a wig?
Enid No!

Pause

Darren Thought not. Bye!

Darren exits through door Y

Enid sees herself in the mirror. She gasps. She takes off the helmet and hat, discards the helmet and puts on the wig. Then she puts on the hat. She makes for door X, thinks the better of it and makes for door Y. She changes her mind and makes back for the storeroom, but can't get in because of the cupboard. She sees the shower curtains and goes to them. She pulls back the curtains and sees that it is a shower, then pulls the curtains closed again. She looks about the room, wondering what to do. She stops dead and looks at the shower again. She creeps back toward it, opens the curtains, looks at the coffin and closes the curtains again. She turns away, stony faced. Pause. She lets out a blood-curdling scream. She keels over backwards and disappears behind the curtains

CURTAIN

ACT II

The same. Immediately following

Enid is still in the shower, behind the curtains

There is a sudden, terrible scream from Sister Tina, off

Tina runs in through door X. She slams the door behind her. She runs to door Y and exits through it, slamming the door behind her

Millichope enters through door X

Millichope Tina? Tina!!

Millichope exits through door Y

Barbara enters through door X

Barbara Rex?

Vanessa enters through door Y

Vanessa Cherry?
Barbara Oh, Doctor, Doctor! Have you seen my husband?

Cherry enters through door X

Cherry Vanessa?
Barbara No — Rex. Cherry?! You're here! I told her you'd gone.
Vanessa Told who?
Cherry And when?
Barbara She was something to do with the something something chickens.
Cherry The Southern Fried Chickens?
Barbara That's it! Who are they?
Cherry I've never heard of them. Sorry.
Barbara Then I'm right! She's incognito!
Vanessa You said she was a Chicken.

Cherry That must be why she went!
Barbara The Chickens have *gone*?
Cherry I can't believe our luck!
Vanessa Don't count your chickens.
Barbara The pale peach pancake! The pragmatic lips! Yes! She almost
certainly was who I think she possibly might be.
Vanessa ⎫
⎬ (*together*) What?
Cherry ⎭
Rex (*off*) Austin?! Inspector?!
Barbara My husband!
Vanessa Over here!

Vanessa goes to door Y and opens it

Barbara exits through door Y

Cherry I've lost the Singing Telegram!
Vanessa Then find him at once!

Vanessa thrusts Cherry out of door X and slams it after her

Oh! The coffin! Cherry mustn't see it! (*She makes for door Y*) Millichope!
Mother Milli ——

Cherry enters through door Y

Cherry I can't find him anywhere!
Vanessa All right, Cherry! I'll take care of the Telegram — you take care
of the coffin. I mean — the cushions!
Cherry What about Mr Cunningham?
Vanessa He can take care of himself.
Cherry Oh, this whole thing's impossible!
Vanessa Look on the bright side! At least now we've not got the Chickens
to coop with.

Vanessa exits through door Y

Cherry tidies the room

Vanessa enters through door X

Cope with.

Vanessa exits through door X

Cherry gathers up some towels, etc.

The shower curtains part and Enid staggers out (without the guitar, which she leaves behind the curtains)

Cherry hands Enid the towels

Cherry Sling those in there, please.

Enid slings the towels into the shower. Cherry makes for the other towels. Enid makes for door Y. Cherry spins around

Cherry Eeek! Who are you?
Enid (*turning*) My name is Tallulah ——
Cherry Of the Southern Fried Chickens!
Enid What?
Cherry But you can't be!
Enid I am!
Cherry But you've gone!
Enid I don't quite follow.
Barbara (*off*) Rex!
Cherry Then perhaps you need some practice!
Enid Pardon?
Rex (*off*) Austin!
Cherry Walk this way!

Cherry and Enid exit through door Y

Barbara enters through door Y

Rex enters through door X with his newt photograph

Barbara Rex!

They embrace

Oh, I've been so worried! It was what the psychiatrist said.
Rex Austin! Where is he? I must see him at once!
Barbara You can't. He isn't here.

Rex Are you sure about that?

Barbara Yes — I've just seen him.

Rex Then what am I to do?

Barbara Do? About what?

Rex (*showing her the photo*) Do about this!

Barbara Oh! It's the newt.

Rex You've seen it before?!

Barbara No. But I've heard about it.

Rex Pardon?

Barbara From Austin. He took the photo.

Rex You think I don't know that? The question is — where?

Barbara What?

Rex No — *where*! *Where* did he take it?

Barbara He took it round to you.

Rex Before that, I mean!

Barbara I don't understand.

Rex Where did he spot these creatures?

Barbara What does it matter where?

Rex The significance of the species! He surely must have known?

Barbara Oh, I don't think he did.

Rex Didn't he?

Barbara No.

Rex Then I don't understand.

Barbara Shall we form a club?

Rex If he didn't know what he'd taken, then why did he take it to me?

Barbara To enter the competition.

Rex Are you saying ... ?

Barbara Yes, I think so.

Rex Barbara! I love you! Do you know what this means?!

Barbara We'll have to get married?

Rex Thank goodness I made that phone call! It was a gamble — but now it's paid off!

Barbara Phone call? Gamble? Paid off? Pardon?

Rex Amphibious Spangulatos! The Greater Spangled Newt!

Barbara What?

Rex It's the rarest newt in the world, you see! In all Great Britain, in actual fact.

Barbara Is it?

Rex Yes! It's protected! And wherever it's located also becomes so! See?!

Barbara Say it to me slowly.

Rex These newts, *and* their territory, are protected by law. No-one can disturb them in any way, shape or form. So — with Amphibious Spangulatos somewhere in this village, the bypass, Barbara, will simply have to be scrapped!

Barbara You mean the village is saved? Oh, Rex — this is wonderful!

Barbara hugs Rex, then freezes

Just a minute, Rex. How do you know they're here?

Rex What?

Barbara Here. In this village. Amphibious Spangulatos.

Rex Austin took this photo to enter the competition.

Barbara Yes.

Rex Well, there you are then.

Barbara D'you think you could explain?

Rex The radius rule! The two-mile radius!

Barbara Oh, yes! Oh, no ——

Rex All photographs entered ——

Barbara Must have been taken within it.

Rex Which means, of course, Barbara ——

Barbara You think those newts are *here.*

Rex Think?! It's *definite*! Barbara? What is it?

Barbara Oh, nothing, Rex! Nothing! No, no! Nothing at all! How many miles does their territory extend?

Rex Amphibious Spangulatos? Oh — about five.

Barbara Miles?

Rex No, yards!

Barbara Yards?!

Rex We're *very* lucky. A colony on our doorstep!

Barbara What if it wasn't?

Rex What?

Barbara Not quite on our doorstep.

Rex Not quite on our doorstep?

Barbara No — but nearly almost.

Rex Pardon?

Barbara I mean ... What if these newts were in ... Chieveley for instance?

Rex Chieveley?

Barbara Just for instance.

Rex Oh, that would be dire!

Barbara Dire?!

Rex Absolutely! Chieveley, you see, must be ——

Barbara Twenty miles away.

Rex Quite.

Barbara (*under her breath*) Oh, this is appalling ...

Rex Pardon?

Barbara What?

Rex Did you say something, Barbara?

Barbara Rex ——

Rex Or am I hearing voices?

Barbara — there's something I've got to tell you. You see ... Voices?! Voices?! Oh, Rex my dearest darling! (*She grabs Rex*)

Rex (*struggling free*) Let go, Barbara! I must speak to Austin!

Barbara Must you?

Rex I must! But we haven't a moment to lose!

Barbara What?

Rex I telephoned the Commission before I left the house.

Barbara Commission? What Commission?

Rex The Wildlife Commission! They're sending an Inspector!

Barbara An Inspector? Here? Tonight?!

Voice (*off*) Austin!

Rex Oh!

Another Voice (*off*) Howzat!

Rex Austin!

Rex makes to exit. Barbara grabs him

Barbara No, Rex! You mustn't!

Rex What?

Barbara Let me go instead!

Rex Pardon?

Barbara sees the cricket helmet and pulls it on

Barbara It's dangerous out there! Cricket balls are flying like missiles on the Somme!

Rex Oh, don't be absurd!

Barbara Please, Rex! Please! I'll tell him what to tell you — then bring him back in here.

Rex Tell him what to tell me?

Barbara I mean — I'll bring him back in here and then he can tell you everything!

Rex Out of my way!

Door Y opens. Vanessa enters

Vanessa Stand back! Stand back! Concussion coming through!

The Protest Group enter; Bradley Cabin, Kirk Maggerty, Muriel Yig, Richard Turnstile, Rosalynde Manchester and Benny Thrower. They are carrying a variety of placards; "Victory to this village!", "Bypass bypassed!", etc. They are also supporting a staggering, semi-conscious Austin. There is a struggle, with people ad libbing accordingly. Rex tries to fight past Vanessa and the Protest Group. Barbara tries to arrest Rex. Eventually Rex gets to the door. The Protest Group and Austin are now well into the room

Rex I must speak to Austin!

Rex exits through door Y

Barbara Rex! Come back!

Barbara exits through door Y

Rosalynde Now — what about our rehearsal?
Vanessa Rehearsal?
Muriel For our Pageant.
Kirk We must see Cherry.

Barbara enters through door Y

Barbara Did I see Austin?!
Muriel He's been hit on the head.
Benny By a very hard ball.

Cherry enters through door Y

Cherry Vanessa!

Rex enters through door Y

Rex Austin!
Barbara Rex!
Rex Not now, Barbara! (*Moving towards Austin*) Austin! This is Rex! Talk to me! Over!
Kirk I'm afraid he's right out.
Rex Out? Then get him in!
Richard In? In where?

Rex The shower, of course! A blast of cold water. Turn it on, Cherry.

Cherry makes for the shower

Vanessa } *(grabbing Cherry and speaking together)* No!!
Barbara
Rex Why not?
Vanessa Erm ... the plumbing's gone wrong.
Barbara Yes!
Cherry What?
Vanessa Absolutely!
Rex Pardon?
Barbara Bring him round too suddenly and he might go into a coma.
Vanessa Coma. That's right.
Rex I've never heard such nonsense!
Barbara Don't argue! She's a psychiatrist!
Rex A psychiatrist! Is this true?
Barbara Yes!
Cherry What?
Vanessa Absolutely!
Cherry Pardon?
Rex But earlier on you were driving a cab.
Barbara A cab? Is this true?
Rex Yes.
Barbara What?
Rex Absolutely!
Cherry Pardon?
Barbara But earlier on you said you were a psychiatrist?
Rex A psychiatrist? Is this true?
Vanessa Yes!
Cherry What?
Vanessa Absolutely!
Rex Pardon?
Vanessa I've been to college. Done a course.
Rex But there hasn't been time.
Vanessa It was a part-time course.
Austin Rex ... ? Rex ... ? Did you want to speak to me? Over.
Rex Yes!
Austin What?
Rex Absolutely!
Austin Pardon?
Rex Come in, Austin! This is Rex! Over!

Austin groans and collapses

Vanessa Get him to the nursery!
Cherry What?
Vanessa Shakespeare.
Cherry Never heard of him.
Vanessa The nursery! The fold-up bed.
Barbara He needs to lie down.
Cherry And then will he come round?
Vanessa Yes. And probably back again.
Rex Back again?
Vanessa To consciousness.
Barbara What?! But he can't!
Cherry Don't argue! She's a psychiatrist!

Rex drags Austin toward door Y

Rex Oh, help me someone! I'm losing my grip!
Vanessa *You're* losing your grip?!

Bradley, Muriel, Kirk and Benny dash to help Rex (they all ad lib)

*Rex, Bradley, Muriel, Kirk and Benny (all carrying Austin and ad libbing)
exit through door Y*

Barbara Rex! Come back!

Barbara exits through door Y

Zandra, who is supporting Keith, enters through door X

Zandra Can we come in, now?
Vanessa No! Get out! Get out!

*Vanessa thrusts Zandra and Keith out of door X and falls out of the door
with them*

Cherry slams the door after them

Rosalynde What was that?
Cherry No — what's this pageant?

Richard Our Victory Pageant.
Rosalynde Because of the bypass.
Rosalynde We need to run through it.
Cherry The bypass?
Richard No — the Pageant.
Rosalynde Rex said you'd help us.
Richard With somewhere to rehearse.
Cherry It'll have to be the cloakroom.
Rosalynde No — it's full of women.
Cherry What?!
Richard They've come for a Hen night.
Cherry But they can't have! Not yet!

Cherry, Richard and Rosalynde exit through door X

Door Y opens. Pybus, Small-Change, Howe, Litmus and Beaverbrook enter

Beaverbrook Sisters — the coffin!
Litmus What coffin?
Beaverbrook Pardon? Oh! Where is it?
Howe (*pointing at the end of the coffin, which sticks out of the shower*) Look, Sisters! Look!

The nuns move towards the shower. Beaverbrook pulls back the curtains. They all look in at the empty coffin. They give a collective gasp

Pybus Mother Enid!
Small-Change Gone!
Howe Oh! (*She holds up the guitar*) Musical grave-robbers! Oh, what shall we do?!
Small-Change We must seek out Mother Millichope and solicit her spiritual guidance!
Pybus We can't find Mother Millichope!
Small-Change Then we'll have to phone the fuzz!

Howe puts down the guitar and the nuns exit through door X

Barbara enters through door Y, supporting Austin

Barbara shifts the guitar and sits Austin down

Barbara Austin! Austin! Are you receiving me? Over!
Austin (*groggy*) Rex?
Barbara No — Barbara!
Austin What do you want?
Barbara To talk to you, Austin.
Austin But why have you brought me here?
Barbara Because you mustn't to Rex.
Austin I mustn't to Rex?
Barbara Talk to him, I mean.
Austin What?
Barbara About the newts.
Austin Mustn't I?
Barbara No. Not until I've told you.
Austin Told me? Told me what?
Barbara Told you where they are.
Austin But I know where they are. Those newts are up at Chieveley.
Barbara No — they're in this village.
Austin No — they're up at Chieveley!
Barbara No — they're in this village!
Austin Barbara! Barbara! Are you feeling quite all right?
Barbara Of course I'm all right! It's you who's got it wrong!
Austin Me? Wrong?
Barbara Yes!
Austin No!
Barbara Don't argue!
Austin But I'm a psychiatrist!
Barbara Right!

She grabs the guitar. Austin gasps

  Where are those newts?!
Austin (*standing defiantly*) Chieveley! Chieveley!

Barbara hits Austin on the head with the guitar. Austin goes rigid

Barbara I'm so sorry, Austin — but I can't take any risks.

*Barbara takes out a handkerchief and wipes her fingerprints from the guitar.
She goes to the shower and puts the guitar in it. Austin starts to fall*

  Rex enters through door Y

Rex Barbara? Barbara!
Barbara Catch him! He's collapsing!

Rex darts to Austin and catches him

Rex What's happened?
Barbara He's collapsed.
Rex Austin! Austin! Where are those newts?!
Austin Barbara ... guitar ... talk to him ... I mustn't ...
Rex Barbara guitar talk to him I mustn't?
Barbara I'm afraid he's quite delirious. Back to the fold-up bed!

*Barbara takes Austin's feet, Rex takes his shoulders, and they carry him
out through door Y*

Vanessa enters through door X. Millichope enters after her

Vanessa pulls back the shower curtain, revealing the coffin

Vanessa Right, you — get it shifted!
Cherry (*off*) Vanessa!
Vanessa Eeek! In here!

She thrusts Millichope into the shower

And don't say a word!

*She pulls the shower curtains closed and moves towards door Y. Millichope
comes out of the shower with the guitar*

Millichope Whose is this?
Vanessa (*grabbing the guitar*) I said keep quiet!

She hits Millichope on the head with the guitar

Millichope Argh.

*Millichope collapses into the shower. Vanessa slings the guitar into the
shower after her and pulls the curtains shut*

Cherry enters through door Y

Cherry Vanessa!
Vanessa Cherry!

Zandra enters through door X, supporting Keith

Zandra I'm getting very tired ——
Vanessa Then have a lie down!

Vanessa slams the door on them, hitting Keith on the head

There is a yell from Keith, off

Cherry Vanessa ——
Vanessa Trust me!
Cherry Trust you?! Trust you?! There's the Protest Group rehearsing a Pageant, Rex running round looking for the Police, Zandra and the Telegram concussed in the corridor, and a gaggle of Hens getting ready in the cloakroom!
Vanessa So — things are a little complicated?
Cherry Complicated? Complicated? Do you know who I found in here just now?
Vanessa This isn't the time for a quiz!
Cherry Her name was Tallulah!
Vanessa Of the Southern Fried Chickens?! But I thought they'd gone?
Cherry She has.
Vanessa Oh, this is awful! Pardon?
Cherry I stuffed her in a taxi.
Vanessa Excellent, Cherry! Now, Zandra wants somewhere to hide the Singing Telegram ...
Cherry Excellent, Cherry?
Vanessa Ah! (*She goes to the cupboard*) The cupboard!
Cherry (*making to door X*) I've had enough!
Vanessa Cherry!
Cherry No! (*She opens door X*)

Zandra, supporting Keith, attempts to enter

Zandra I can't keep lugging ——
Cherry Argh!

Cherry slams the door on them, hitting Keith in the face

There is a groan from Keith, off

Cherry exits through door Y

Vanessa makes for door Y

Vanessa Cherry!

Keith enters through door X

Keith I want my mother!
Vanessa Argh!

She dashes toward Keith. Millichope comes out of the shower looking bedraggled. She has the guitar

Millichope Did somebody call?
Vanessa What?

Millichope strums the guitar and sings

Millichope "He's got the whole world in his hands!"
Millichope } *(together)* "He's got the whole wide world ——"
Keith

Vanessa snatches the guitar from Millichope

Vanessa Shut up! Shut up!
Keith "— in his hands!"

Vanessa hits Keith on the head with the guitar

Keith yells and falls out of door Y

Vanessa slams the door after him

Millichope Who was that?
Vanessa No-one! Shift that coffin!
Millichope I can't! Not on my own!
Vanessa *(brandishing the guitar)* Then go and get Sister Tina!

Millichope runs to door X. Vanessa gives chase, brandishing the guitar

Door X opens and Enid enters

Millichope Out of my way!

Millichope exits through door X and slams it behind her

Enid (*taking the guitar from Vanessa*) Ah! That's what I came back for!
Vanessa Oh, I wondered whose it was. Eeek! Who are you?
Enid My name is Tallulah!
Vanessa Of the Southern Fried Chickens?!
Enid Has someone been talking?
Vanessa (*grabbing Enid*) Out of here! Out of here!

She drags Enid to door X

Door X opens and Zandra enters

Zandra The Policeman's ——
Enid Policeman?!
Vanessa I'm sorry — he's not home yet!
Zandra What?
Vanessa Not until this evening!

Vanessa thrusts Zandra out through door X and slams it after her

She drags Enid to door Y

Door Y opens and Keith steps in

Keith Evening all!
Enid Argh!

Vanessa slams the door on Keith

Enid dives into the cupboard

Vanessa (*grabbing Enid*) Get out! Get out! You can't stay in there!
Enid But I've got to! They mustn't find me!
Vanessa All right, then — but keep it shut!
Enid What?
Vanessa (*pointing to a handle on the inside of the door*) The handle! The handle! (*She slams the cupboard door*) Cherry? Cherry!

Vanessa exits through door Y

Millichope and Tina enter through door X

Tina But what about the law? It's a wicked thing we're doing!
Millichope (*moving to the shower*) Wicked? Oh, don't be ... law?
Tina I can feel that policeman's fingers clutching at me now!
Millichope (*pulling the shower curtains open*) I told you, Sister Tina — there *isn't* a policeman!
Tina But there is, Mother Millichope! You said so yourself!

Tina makes for door Y and opens it

Millichope Tina!

Tina — looking off — shrieks and slams door Y

Tina runs to door X and exits

What ... ? (*She pulls the shower curtains closed*) Tina!

Millichope exits through door X

Cherry and Zandra, supporting Keith, enter through door Y. Keith clutches his sports bag

Cherry (*making for the cupboard*) Right — over here! And this is the last thing I'm doing!
Zandra What?

Vanessa dashes in through door Y

Vanessa Cherry! Not the cupboard!
Zandra Exactly.
Vanessa Pardon?
Zandra Well, it's no good to me stuck in that corner. I want the guests to see him when he jumps out for his song.
Cherry All right then — the shower.
Vanessa Yes. (*Grabbing Keith*) I mean — no!
Zandra Pardon?
Vanessa I mean — not yet.

Cherry What?
Vanessa Erm ... We've got to discuss the cocktails!
Zandra Cocktails?
Vanessa Yes, cocktails!

Vanessa pushes Keith into Zandra. Zandra gasps

Cherry Vanessa!
Vanessa (*under her breath*) Over here!

Zandra struggles with Keith and with his bag. Vanessa drags Cherry to the cupboard, and jerks her head at it. She makes clucking noises and "flaps" her arms. Cherry looks bewildered. Vanessa is desperate. She breaks out in an uninhibited chicken routine, flapping about the room and clucking at full pitch. Zandra stares in disbelief. Noticing this, Vanessa alters her behaviour so that it seems as if she is looking for a key in her clothes. Eventually, she dries up, and stops, embarrassed. Zandra and Cherry exchange glances

> *Behind them all, Keith staggers to his feet and exits, dazed, through door X*

Zandra What do you think you're playing at?
Vanessa Looking for the key!
Zandra What?
Vanessa The key! For the cupboard! Cherry?
Cherry Yes?
Barbara Where is it?
Cherry I don't know what you're talking about.
Vanessa Well why did you leave it there?
Cherry Pardon?
Vanessa (*under her breath*) Come on! We've got to talk!

Vanessa drags Cherry out through door X

Zandra Keith. Keith?

> *Keith enters through door Y, singing and dancing*

Keith (*singing*)   "... Like this Chrissy,
                    Like no Chrissy we know!
                    Chrissy's getting married in the morning!
                    So I've come here ———"

Zandra Yes. Lovely. Thank you. Get in the cupboard.
Keith But what about my cue?
Zandra Cue?
Keith To jump out.
Zandra Oh, yes. Screwdriver!
Keith Pardon?
Zandra We're going to have some cocktails.
Keith Cocktails?
Zandra Apparently. Now, Christina's favourite cocktail ——
Keith Christina?
Zandra That's her name.
Keith You said it was *Chrissy*. I've worked it into the song!
Zandra Well, you'll have to work it out again!
Keith It'll mean an abbreviation.
Zandra No — just shorten her name.
Keith What?
Zandra Now — when I mention "screwdriver" you jump out of the
cupboard.
Keith Screwdriver?
Zandra Right.
Keith Jump?
Zandra When you hear it. Oh, and can you work in a "wicked"?
Keith Pardon?
Zandra "Wicked". The word. It's her favourite, you see. Wicked this,
wicked that. Do it when you arrest her.
Keith Right. (*He makes for the cupboard*) Oh, I haven't got my costume!
Zandra And I haven't got the key.
Keith Pardon?
Zandra And it's still in the corner.
Keith What?
Zandra Back in a minute.

Zandra exits through door Y

*Keith looks about, dazed and bewildered. He sees the bag, takes it and pulls
out his uniform. He begins to strip off his track suit when he hears the voices
of Vanessa and Cherry, off. He dashes to the cupboard. He does the action
of opening the door (but of course it doesn't open since Enid is holding it on
the inside) and dives "in". He hits his head on the cupboard and yells. He
staggers back and dives into the shower. He wails and staggers out of the
shower, holding the coffin lid and rubbing his head. He puts the lid against
the wall. He looks at the lid, then at the shower and creeps, gingerly, towards*

it to pull the curtains open a fraction. He peeks in. He gasps and faints, collapsing into the shower so that he is hidden by the curtains

Vanessa and Cherry enter through door Y

Vanessa dashes to the cupboard

Cherry (*making for the shower*) Are you seriously trying to tell me the dead one's still in there?

Vanessa (*grabbing Cherry*) Never mind the nuns! We've got to get rid of Tallulah! (*Knocking at the cupboard door*) Open up! It's me!

Barbara enters through door X, holding a cricket bat

Barbara Cherry?

Vanessa slams the cupboard door

Vanessa }
Cherry } (*together*) Yes!

Barbara Get that shower mended. They'll be here any minute.

Vanessa }
Cherry } (*together*) Who?

Barbara The cricketers of course. Austin's in a coma. I've told them the match is off.

Cherry Argh!

Cherry exits through door X. Vanessa goes after her

Vanessa Cherry!

Vanessa exits through door X

Barbara (*moving to door X*) Come back! Oh ... (*She moves to the shower*)

Rex enters through door Y

Rex Barbara! Quickly! The Inspector's arrived!
Barbara Inspector!
Rex Yes!
Barbara What has he said?

Rex The Inspector?
Barbara No — Austin!
Rex Nothing. Not yet. But he's coming round fast!
Barbara Where's that guitar?
Rex Pardon?
Barbara (*remembering the bat; looking at it*) Oh, I'll improvise!

Barbara exits through door Y

Rex Barbara? Barbara!

Rex exits through door Y

Millichope and Tina enter through door Y

Millichope Where did you put the lid?
Tina You had it last!

Millichope makes for door X

Don't leave me, Mother Millichope!
Millichope Keep calm, Tina!
Tina Calm! How can I?!
Millichope Look for the posi-drive! That should do the trick.

Millichope exits through door X

Tina Oh, this is appalling! Just ... (*She notices the lid*) The lid! (*She dashes to door X and opens it*) Mother Milli ...

There is a groan from Keith in the shower. Tina spins round and listens. Silence. She closes door X

Keep calm, Tina. That's all you have to do. Ah! (*She picks up Millichope's screwdriver from Act I*) The screwdriver!

She takes hold of the lid, with her back to the shower. The curtains part, revealing Keith in a PC uniform

Keith Screwdriver!

Tina freezes, clutching the lid

(*Striding forward*) Tina! Wicked Tina!

Tina squeaks

Oh, wicked, wicked, *wicked* Tina!

Tina groans

Keith I arrest you, *wicked* Tina ... In the name of the law!

Keith plants his hand on Tina's shoulder. Tina looks at it, appalled. She screams and spins round, making to escape. The lid hits Keith in the face. He reels back with a groan and staggers about the room ludicrously. He falls into the shower and collapses into the coffin. Tina is aghast. She goes to the shower, looks at Keith in the coffin and places the lid on top of him. She closes the curtains. She crosses herself. Pause. She screams and makes for door X

Door X opens and Millichope enters

Millichope Tina! What is it?
Tina (*pointing at shower*) The policeman! I've killed him!
Millichope What?!
Tina Oh, banged up for murder — and never took my vows!

Millichope pulls back curtains and lifts the lid from the coffin

Millichope He's only unconscious!
Tina What? Oh, a miracle!

Millichope pulls Keith out of the coffin and struggles forward with him

Millichope Take him! Take him!

She hands Keith to Tina

Barbara (*off*) This way, Inspector!
Millichope Inspector!
Tina Argh!

Tina exits, with Keith, through door X. She leaves the screwdriver

*Millichope makes to follow then realizes she has left the shower curtains
open. She dashes back and just as she gets there, door Y begins to open.
Millichope darts into the shower, pulling the curtains closed. (NB: Millichope
gets into the coffin and puts on the lid)*

Barbara enters through door Y, accompanied by Inspector Sheridan

Barbara I'm sorry about my husband's confusion. We're expecting an
Inspector you see, Inspector.
Sheridan But I am an Inspector.
Barbara Chief Inspector Sheridan.
Sheridan Of the Berkshire Police.
Barbara Quite.
Sheridan I beg your pardon?
Barbara You're nothing to do with newts.
Sheridan Newts? Newts? It's far more serious than newts!

PC Carpenter enters through door Y

Carpenter I've located the nuns, sir. They're working on the hearse.
Barbara Nuns? Hearse? What's all this about?
Sheridan We happened to be in the area when the emergency call came
through.
Barbara Emergency call?
Sheridan From a phone box.
Barbara I don't quite understand.
Sheridan Neither do I.
Carpenter Their money ran out.
Sheridan But I think I got the gist. The said nuns, apparently, seem to have
lost a body. Or rather, it's been stolen.
Barbara A body?
Sheridan Yes, a body — (*he produces a certificate*) which you, Dr
Cunningham, have recently certified dead.
Barbara Mother Superior Enid? But surely she's buried by now?
Carpenter It would seem not, madam.
Sheridan (*putting away the certificate*) Mind if we have a shufty?
Barbara You won't find anything here.
Sheridan Carpenter — take the shower.
Carpenter But I had a bath last week.
Sheridan *Look* in the shower, Carpenter!

Carpenter goes into the shower. Sheridan makes for the cupboard

What's this, madam?
Barbara A completely empty cupboard.

Enid steps out, slamming the door behind her

Enid My name is Tallulah!
Barbara Of the Southern Fried Chickens!
Sheridan You know this lady, Doctor?
Carpenter (*from behind shower curtains*) Sir! Inspector Sheridan!

Sheridan goes to the shower. Enid makes to exit

Barbara (*grabbing Enid*) Just a minute, you! Let me see those lips!

Carpenter pulls back the curtains to reveal the coffin, with the lid on

Carpenter Look, sir!
Enid Eeek!
Carpenter Yes! (*He points at the ceiling*) It's a skylight!
Sheridan Over here, please madams.

Enid tries to escape

Barbara (*dragging Enid to the shower*) Oh, no you don't!
Sheridan Draw the curtains, Carpenter.
Carpenter Sir?
Sheridan I'm going to remove the lid.
Carpenter (*seeing the coffin*) Oh! A coffin!

Sheridan pulls the curtains shut (Sheridan, Carpenter, Enid and Barbara are now hidden in the shower)

   Bradley and Benny enter through door X. Bradley carries a huge dragon costume. It's a Chinese dragon-type affair, but very Anglicized. As he enters, he is stuffing it into a bag, but the head remains visible

Benny Careful, careful! That bag's got a rip in it!
Bradley Don't get in a state!

Benny (*showing him the bag*) No — it's falling to bits, look.
Bradley Yes, yes, yes ——
Benny Oh, I hope it'll be all right.
Bradley The bag?
Benny No — the Pageant!
Bradley The Pageant'll be spectacular! St George and the Dragon! What could be better for defeating the bypass?
Benny We could do with a bit more rehearsal, really. And a few more people.
Bradley What?
Benny For the Dragon, I mean. That costume's enormous!
Bradley Everything's going to be fine!

Bradley opens the cupboard

Benny You can't leave it there!
Bradley We're coming back first thing!
Bradley But ——

Bradley hangs the bag on a hook on the inside of the door and closes the cupboard

There we are! Come on.

Benny and Bradley exit through door X

Cherry and Vanessa enter through door Y

Vanessa We've got to get her out!
Cherry But someone might see her!
Vanessa No-one'll see her! As soon as the Telegram's finished we'll put her straight back in!
Cherry What about the other four?
Vanessa Other four?
Cherry They're a five-piece band!
Vanessa Oh, you mean the Chickens? No — there wouldn't be room.
Cherry What?
Vanessa In the cupboard.
Cherry Pardon?

Vanessa looks in the cupboard

Vanessa Oh, I don't know. With a bit of a squash —— Eek!

Cherry What?
Vanessa Tallulah! She's gone!
Cherry Gone!? Gone where?!
Vanessa I don't know, Cherry! (*She slams the door closed*) But it's one less thing to worry about.
Cherry (*making to leave*) No! We've got to find her!
Vanessa (*grabbing Cherry*) In a minute! In a minute!

She drags Cherry to the cupboard

Vanessa (*pointing*) Right against that wall.
Cherry Pardon?
Vanessa Well, that's where Zandra wants it. Now — one two ——
Cherry Buckle my shoe.

With a groan they push the cupboard into the middle of the room

> *The door of the store room is thrown open and Lolita, Blanche, Aramist and Cyd burst out. They are now in their cowgirl gear. They screech and wail, gasping for breath. They run out of the room, severally*

Cherry looks at Vanessa and screams

Vanessa Cherry!

Cherry runs to door Y. Vanessa makes after her, then remembers the cupboard. She goes back to it

> *Cherry opens door Y and Zandra attempts to come in*

Zandra Have you found that key, yet?
Cherry Argh!

> *Cherry slams the door in Zandra's face*

There is a shriek from Zandra, off

Vanessa Cherry!

> *Cherry exits through door X, slamming the door behind her*

Vanessa pushes the cupboard against the wall near door Y. She makes after Cherry

(NB: stage management should now open the false panel in the wall near door Y and the doors in the back of the cupboard)

Vanessa pulls open door X

Vanessa Cherry!

  Door Y opens and Cherry enters

Cherry They're coming! They're coming!
Vanessa The cupboard!
Cherry What?!
Vanessa *(propelling Cherry to the cupboard)* Open it! Open it!
Cherry It's stuck! It's stuck!

Vanessa dashes to door X and slams it closed

  The Chickens run in through door Y, leaving the door open behind them. They make to door X

Vanessa throws up her arms, signalling to the Chickens

Vanessa Diversion! Diversion!

The Chickens swing round and head for the cupboard. Cherry shrieks. She makes a final, desperate, violent tug at the cupboard door. The door springs open and Cherry dives aside

  The Chickens pile into the cupboard (and, of course, exit through the fake wall)

Vanessa dashes to the cupboard and slams the door after them. Cherry runs to door X

  Done it!

  Cherry exits through door X, slamming the door behind her

(Hearing the door) Cherry? Cherry!

Vanessa exits through door X

(NB: stage management should now close the hidden doors in the wall and the cupboard)

Tina, supporting Keith, enters through door Y

She looks about the room, then goes to the cupboard and tries to open it, but can't. She looks about again, then goes to the storeroom, taking Keith

She puts Keith in the storeroom and closes the door after him

Sheridan *(from inside the shower)* Then perhaps a little more light would help?
Tina Eeek!
Sheridan Sergeant!
Tina Sergeant?
Sheridan The coffin!
Tina Argh!

Tina exits through door Y

The shower curtains are drawn back by Sheridan. Carpenter pushes the trolley (with the coffin on it) into the room (the lid is left in the shower). Barbara, Enid, Sheridan and Carpenter gather around the coffin

Sheridan Now then, madam — shall we try again? Is this, or is this not, the body of the woman you certified dead?
Barbara I told you, Inspector; I can't be sure.
Sheridan Then take a closer look. Carpenter!
Carpenter Sir!

Carpenter lifts Millichope by the shoulders, making her visible to both Barbara and the audience. Barbara looks closely at Millichope, then looks at Enid, then turns to Sheridan

Barbara Yes. It is.
Sheridan And you're quite sure she's dead?
Barbara Quite sure, Inspector.

Sheridan So she couldn't have got up and left this coffin a moment?
Barbara Impossible, I assure you. That nun's as dead as a doornail.
Sheridan Thank you, Doctor Cunningham. Carpenter!
Carpenter Sir!

Carpenter replaces Millichope, gets the lid from the shower and screws it on to the coffin with Millichope's screwdriver

Sheridan You've been most helpful, madam. I can now, with absolute confidence, close both case and coffin. (*He puts down the screwdriver*)
Carpenter Oh, very good sir. Case *and* coffin. Ha ha! Most amusing.
Sheridan Yes, thank you, Carpenter. Lead me to the Sisters.
Carpenter Sir!

Sheridan and Carpenter exit through door X

Enid Oh, thank you so much! What can I say?
Barbara Amphibious Spangulatos.
Enid No — that's a bit of a mouthful.
Vanessa Up at your convent! Or rather, in the mud. The mud of the pond.
Enid I don't understand.
Barbara You must fetch me some at once.
Enid Go back to the convent?!
Barbara And get me some mud!
Enid Impossible! Impossible!
Barbara For me, perhaps, yes. But not for you — (*she snatches off Enid's wig*) Mother Superior Enid!
Enid Oh!
Barbara Well, that's your name, isn't it? I don't know what you're up to, and I don't much care, but refuse to help me, Enid, and I'll shop you to the police!
Enid I *can't* fetch that mud!
Barbara Of course you can! It's easy! I'll equip you with some bin bags.

Rex enters through door Y

Rex Barbara! Barbara! Austin's coming round!
Barbara What?!
Rex Hallo. Who are you?
Barbara Her name is ... Tallulah.
Enid Of the Southern Fried Chickens!
Rex Where's that, Inspector?

Barbara I sent him back to you.
Rex What?! To the nursery?! Austin! Austin!

Rex exits through door Y

Barbara Get that mud!
Enid But ——
Barbara (*pointing at door X*) The bags are in the kitchen!

Barbara exits through door Y

Enid makes for door X. There is banging from inside the coffin. Enid goes to the coffin and tugs at the lid

Enid Oh ... where's that screwdriver?!

Keith comes out of the storeroom

Keith Screwdriver!
Enid Argh!

Enid dives under the trolley so that she is hidden by the cloth. The coffin lid flies open and hits Keith in the face. Keith yells and collapses. Millichope sits up, gasping for breath

Millichope Get me out! Get me out!

Enid comes out from under the trolley. Keith crawls under it from the other side, clutching the lid

Enid Where's that policeman?!
Millichope There isn't a policeman! (*Struggling from the coffin*) Will you get me *out*!
Enid I can't get you out! I've got to get the mud!
Millichope Mud? What mud?!
Enid From the pond at the convent!
Millichope Convent pond mud? There's bags of it in the shower.
Enid What?!
Millichope Well, I had to use something to weigh down the coffin! The mud from the pond was the nearest thing to hand!

There is a great chant from the nuns, off. Millichope wails. Enid thrusts the trolley back into the shower (thus revealing Keith underneath the trolley). Keith staggers to his feet, holding the lid

The lid! The lid!

There is more chanting from the nuns. Millichope pulls the shower curtains closed. Enid turns to Keith

Keith Here we are. (*He offers the lid*)
Enid (*taking it*) Thank you. Eeek!

She swings around with the lid and hits Keith in the face. Keith collapses. Enid goes into the shower with the lid (NB: Enid and Millichope now exchange clothes and Enid gets into the coffin)

Carpenter enters through door X

Carpenter This way, Sisters! Oh. How did I get down there? (*He kneels down to see to Keith*)

Sheridan enters through door X

Sheridan Carpenter!
Carpenter Sir!
Sheridan What are you doing?
Carpenter Seeing to this, sir.
Sheridan What is it?
Carpenter Me.
Sheridan Asleep on duty? Have you been drinking?

Carpenter smells Keith's breath

Carpenter No, I don't think so.
Sheridan Then I'm prepared, in this instance, to forgive and forget.
Carpenter (*standing and saluting*) Thank you so much, sir! You've a very sweet nature.
Sheridan Where's Dr Cunningham — and the Southern Fried Chickens?
Carpenter They seem to have gone.
Sheridan Then we'll have to manage alone.

Carpenter Sir!

Sheridan exits through door X

Carpenter goes to the shower and pulls the curtains open. Millichope is seen, dressed as Tallulah and pulling on the wig. On top of the coffin is the bag of mud. Carpenter doesn't see any of this as he is dealing with the curtains. Millichope sees Carpenter and, grabbing the bag of mud, she darts under the trolley. Carpenter goes to the rear of the trolley and tries pushing it but it won't budge. He puts his back to the trolley (he cannot, now, see the room)

Zandra enters through door Y

She sees Keith, goes to him and kneels. She tries to lift Keith and as she does this, Carpenter gives a great shove at the trolley. It moves forward. Keith and Zandra see this. They freeze and the trolley comes towards them, covering them so that they are hidden underneath. Carpenter stops and looks about. He can't see anything. He makes for door X. Noticing that the coffin lid is loose, he finds Millichope's screwdriver and screws it down. He satisfies himself that the lid is well and truly on. The nuns sing, off

Beaverbrook, Pybus, Howe, Litmus, and Small-Change enter through door Y. They gather around the coffin

Sheridan enters with Tina through door X

Tina No! No!
Sheridan But the body hasn't gone, madam. It's still in the coffin. That's what we want to show you.
Tina Still in the coffin? You think I believe that?
Sheridan Carpenter — the lid!
Carpenter Sir!

Carpenter produces the screwdriver and removes the lid. All the nuns gasp. Tina wails and makes for door X

Nuns Mother Enid!
Tina (*turning back*) Pardon?

Everyone looks at Tina. Tina goes to the coffin. Carpenter lifts Enid by the shoulders

Tina Oh! Mother Enid!
Sheridan Quite.
Tina And she's dead?
Carpenter As dead as a doornail.
Tina Can this be true?
Sheridan Absolutely, madam. (*Producing a certificate*) She's been certified
   as such by a fully-qualified doctor.
Tina (*grabbing the certificate*) What? Oh ...!

*The other nuns rush to comfort Tina. Carpenter lowers Enid back into the
coffin and replaces the lid, screwing it down. He pulls the shower curtains
closed*

Sheridan Now then, ladies, if you'd like to bring round the hearse — you're
   free to proceed with the funeral. Carpenter and I will escort you on the way.
   Carpenter!
Carpenter Sir!

Everyone exits through door X

*Millichope comes out from under the trolley. She is holding the bag of mud,
but she isn't wearing the wig. She goes to door Y and sees herself in the
mirror. She realizes she is not wearing the wig and doubles back to the coffin.
She puts the bag on top of the coffin and lifts the cloth around the trolley. She
sees that the wig is caught up in Zandra and Keith, who have been underneath
the trolley all this time. She struggles to get the wig*

Millichope Oh! Unconscious! Both of them!

*She gives a violent tug at the wig and it comes free. She pulls it on and, taking
the bag of mud, she makes for door Y. There is banging from inside the coffin.
Millichope goes back to the coffin*

Barbara enters through door Y

Barbara Ah! You've got it!
Millichope Eeek! Dr Cunningham!

*Barbara takes the bag of mud. Millichope pulls at the wig in an effort to hide
her face*

Barbara I must say you, Enid, you were very, very quick.

Millichope Enid? No! My name is Tallulah ——

Barbara Oh, don't start that agai —— Just a minute!

Millichope Pardon?

Barbara Amphibious Spangulatos!

Millichope Oh, you mean the newts.

Barbara Dehydrated completely!

Millichope No — they're only hibernating.

Barbara Hibernating?

Millichope Yes. That's what they do when the pond dries up. Along with the herbs those newts are my special study. I know each and every detail of their natural behaviour.

Barbara Water!

Millichope What?

Barbara And a bucket to sloosh them in!

Millichope That won't work.

Barbara Pardon?

Millichope No — they're catatonic. They'll have gone into their winter cycle, you see? They won't come out for months.

Barbara But the Inspector!

Millichope Inspector?

Barbara Just a minute!

Millichope What?

Barbara I'm a doctor, aren't I? I've free and ready access to artificial stimulants!

Millichope Oh, have you?

Barbara Come with me, Enid! I'll need your advice. I might be a doctor — but I know nothing at all about newts!

Barbara exits through door Y, dragging Millichope with her. She forgets the bag of mud

There is banging from inside the coffin

Tina enters through door X. She carries a screwdriver and the certificate

She creeps to the coffin. She looks at the certificate, then at the coffin. She unscrews the lid. Putting the screwdriver down, she reaches gingerly for the lid. The lid flies open and Enid sits up, gasping for breath. Tina is horrified. She staggers back, holding the lid

Enid Tina? Tina ...

Tina screams and drops the lid

She exits, running, through door X

Enid Tina!
Cherry *(off; from door Y)* Vanessa!

Enid looks at door Y

Vanessa *(off; from door X)* Cherry!

Enid looks at door X and panics. She tries to get the lid but can't reach it. She starts to get out of the coffin but doors X and Y begin to open. Enid throws herself back into the coffin

Cherry enters through door X and Vanessa enters through door Y. They slam the doors behind them

Cherry
Vanessa } *(together)* They're coming! They're coming!

They run to either side of the coffin

Cherry
Vanessa } *(together)* Who are?!
Vanessa The police!
Cherry The Cricketers!
Cherry
Vanessa } *(together)* Eeek!

They grab hands across the coffin. Then they notice what's inside

Cherry
Vanessa } *(together)* Argh!

Off, we hear the sound of the nuns singing

Sheridan *(off; from door X)* Carpenter — the door!
Vanessa *(making for cupboard)* Barricade! Barricade!

Vanessa and Cherry push the cupboard in front of door X

> (*NB: at this point stage management open the false doors in the back of the cupboard and door X. Lolita, Cyd and the other Chickens get into the cupboard*)

Vanessa and Cherry stand with their backs to the cupboard. There is hammering on door X

Sheridan (*off*) Police! Police! Open up in there!

Cherry wails and runs for door Y. Vanessa makes after her. The cupboard door begins to open and Lolita and Cyd squawk out. Vanessa turns and thrusts them back into the cupboard. Cherry opens door Y and screams. She slams the door shut and runs to Vanessa

Cherry The Cricketers! The Cricketers!

Cherry pulls wildly at the cupboard door. It flies open. Blanche and Aramist flail out. Vanessa thrusts them back in and slams the door after them. Vanessa and Cherry stand with their backs against the cupboard door

> *Door Y opens and Roger Bloom runs in*

Vanessa and Cherry gasp and throw their hands over their faces. Roger runs across the room and meets with the coffin

Roger Oops!

He moves around the coffin to the other side, stops, turns back and looks inside it. He gasps and swoons

Vanessa Catch him! Catch him!

Cherry dashes to Roger and catches him as he collapses backwards

> Over here! Quickly!

Cherry hurls Roger towards Vanessa. He bounces off the wall, R. Vanessa opens the cupboard. There is a squawk from the Chickens as Roger bounces into the cupboard. Vanessa slams the door after him

During the above Martin Box enters through door Y, runs round the coffin, looks back in it, swoons and falls. Cherry catches him and hurls him towards Vanessa. He bounces off the wall towards the cupboard, Vanessa opens the cupboard door and slams it after him, etc.

And the next one please!

The rest of the cricket team enter one by one and this sequence of events is repeated, almost mechanically, for each of them

All the while Sheridan hammers on the door, demanding to be let in

At the end of the sequence, after the Cricketers and Chickens have exited through the back, stage management close the false doors in both the cupboard and door X. NB: Lolita stays in the cupboard

Cherry We've got to get out! We've got to get out!

Cherry pulls open the cupboard door. Lolita flails out. Vanessa and Cherry thrust her back in again and slam the door

Vanessa This way! This way!

They dash to door Y. Vanessa opens it, then slams it again

That way! That way!

They dash to the cupboard and push it sideways away from door X, into the shower

Vanessa and Cherry exit through door X

Enid gets out of the coffin and makes to exit. She sees the bag of mud, picks it up, puts it in the coffin and throws on the lid

Enid Tina! Tina!

Enid exits through door X

Sheridan and Carpenter enter through door Y

Sheridan } *(together)* This way, Sisters!
Carpenter }

The nuns enter through door Y. They are singing. They pick up the coffin and exit with it through door X

Carpenter *(going to the cupboard)* This cupboard's been moved.
Sheridan Well observed, Sergeant.
Carpenter It's all very strange. What can be going on?
Sheridan I don't know, Carpenter. But I mean to find out.

Sheridan goes to door X to exit. Carpenter makes to follow

Sheridan Carpenter.
Carpenter Sir?
Sheridan The cupboard.
Carpenter Of course!

Sheridan exits through door X

Carpenter pushes the cupboard against wall Y

NB: stage management now open the false doors in the cupboard and wall

Millichope enters through door Y. She carries a bucket

Carpenter Please — let me help you.
Millichope Oh — thank you very much.

Carpenter takes the bucket and puts it on the trolley. He makes to door X. Millichope realizes that the coffin has gone

Millichope Stop!
Carpenter Madam?
Millichope Where's the coffin?
Carpenter Six foot under. Evening all!

Carpenter exits through door X

Millichope Enid! Buried! Alive!!

Barbara enters through door X. She has a large first aid box

Barbara Right, here we are ... Oh! Where's the mud?!
Millichope Enid! Enid!
Barbara Stop! Come back! I need your expertise!

Millichope exits through door X

Barbara makes after her, then stops. She sees a "newt" on the floor

Oh! (*She kneels down*) Amphibious Spangulatos! (*She picks up the newt and takes it to the bucket and drops it in. She takes some bottles from the first aid box and looks at them. She is unsure. Eventually, she opens all the bottles and tips them into the bucket. She shakes the bucket and sniffs. She is repelled by the smell. The bucket starts to fizz and smoke*) Oh ... ! (*She runs around the room with the bucket. Eventually, she opens the cupboard and slings the bucket in. She slams the door shut and leans against the door*) What have I done?! What have I done?!

There is a great groan from inside the cupboard — it is the Cricketers and Chickens (who are, in fact, behind the wall)

Argh!!!

She runs to door X and opens it. She screams and slams the door shut. She makes for door Y

Cherry and Vanessa enter through door X

Vanessa }
Cherry } (*together*) Barbara?!

Door Y opens. Sheridan, Millichope, and Carpenter enter. Carpenter carries the bag of mud

Sheridan Just one moment, madam!

Cherry and Vanessa shriek and make to exit

Sheridan Stop!

Vanessa } (*together*) What?!
Cherry

Sheridan No-one must leave this room. Carpenter!
Carpenter Sir!

Carpenter gives the bag of mud to Sheridan, goes to door X and stands in front of it

Barbara What is the meaning of this!?
Sheridan On the contrary, madam — what is the meaning of this?! (*He holds up the bag of mud*)
Barbara Oh!
Sheridan So — you recognize the remnants of your terrible deed?
Barbara Terrible deed!
Carpenter Pardon?
Barbara The newts! Just tell me you haven't spoken to Rex! My husband, I swear, knows nothing about it!
Sheridan It would make no difference. In British Law, madam, one spouse cannot testify against another. Which is just as well, really; the courts would be chock-a-block.
Barbara Courts! I'm to be prosecuted?!
Sheridan Produce the body, madam, and the judge might just show leniency.
Barbara The body?! Very well. You'll find it in the bucket.
Carpenter Bucket?
Millichope Oh!
Sheridan A nun squashed, willy-nilly, into a polyurethane tub?!
Millichope What sort of monster are you?!
Barbara Nun?
Sheridan Mother Enid!
Barbara But *she's* Mother Enid!
Millichope No! I'm Mother Millichope!
Barbara No! You're Tallulah! Which means you're Mother Enid!
Barbara But Mother Enid's dead!
Sheridan Quite.
Millichope No — she's alive! That's why I asked you to open the coffin. If you hadn't she would have been!
Carpenter Would have been?
Millichope Dead!
Sheridan But she wasn't in the coffin.
Millichope Exactly — she's in the bucket! We've got to get her out!
Sheridan It's too late for that — she's dead!

Millichope What?
Sheridan (*to Barbara*) Isn't she?
Barbara Yes.
Millichope No! That was me!
Sheridan Pardon?
Millichope In the coffin.
Carpenter No — that was mud.
Millichope Before that, I mean!
Sheridan So — you *are* Mother Enid!
Carpenter Then where's Mother Millichope?
Millichope *I'm* Mother Millichope!
Barbara What?
Millichope Tina, I swear, will testify to it!
Carpenter Tina?
Barbara Who's Tina?

Tina enters through door Y

Tina Millichope! Mother Millichope!
Millichope (*embracing her*) Tina! Tina!
Tina Eeek! Who are you?

Enid enters through door Y

Enid Her name is Tallulah!
Sheridan Of the Southern Fried Chickens?
Carpenter Then where's Mother Enid?
Tina Argh! The policeman!

Tina makes to exit. Barbara grabs her

Barbara If this is Tallulah — then where's Mother Enid?
Tina (*pointing at Enid*) This is Mother Enid!
Barbara But it can't be! She's dead!
Enid No — I'm alive!
Tina Which is why I must see Mother Millichope! Take me to her at once!
Millichope Tina! I'm here!

Millichope pulls off her wig. Everyone gasps. Tina grabs the wig

Sheridan Then where's Tallulah's body?
Barbara What?

Sheridan You spoke of a body!
Carpenter A body in a bucket!
Sheridan A body in the bucket to which you, yourself, confessed!
Barbara No, that's my newt!
Carpenter It must be, to fit in a bucket.
Sheridan Newt! Newt! What do you think I am?
Barbara I think you're about to arrest me.
Sheridan You're making sense at last! Carpenter — the handcuffs!
Tina Wait! Wait! I can explain!
Millichope } (*together*) Tina!
Enid
Tina No! The time has come for Truth!
Millichope } (*together*) Argh!
Enid
Tina (*pointing at Barbara*) This woman is innocent!
Sheridan How do you know?
Tina (*pointing at Enid*) Because *this* one is Tallulah!
Sheridan You said she was Enid!
Tina She was! (*Brandishing it*) Before this wig!
Sheridan Disguise!!
Tina Quite!
Carpenter Oh! So there hasn't been a murder at all in fact?
Sheridan But what about the body?!
Barbara What?
Sheridan The bucket!
Barbara It's Amphibian!
Sheridan What?

Rex and Austin enter through door Y

Rex Inspector! Inspector! This is the vital witness!
Barbara (*throwing herself at Austin*) No, Austin! No!
Sheridan (*grabbing Barbara*) Stand back, madam.
Barbara (*wailing*) But he'll top himself! He'll top himself!
Sheridan Carpenter!
Carpenter Sir!

Carpenter drags the gibbering Barbara to one side

Rex (*making for Barbara*) Barbara ... ?
Sheridan (*to Austin*) Now then, sir. What do you know of this Amphibian?
Austin Nothing, Inspector. Only that it's in Chieveley.

Sheridan Chieveley?
Rex Chieveley?!
Barbara Oh — forgive me, Rex!
Sheridan But I thought it was in the bucket?
Barbara And I thought it was in the bag!
Rex Barbara?
Barbara It's no good, Rex. You have to know the truth.
Rex What?
Barbara Amphibious Spangulatos were never in this village. Austin's
    photograph was taken — at the convent.
Tina   } (*together*) The convent?!
Millichope
Barbara Up at Chieveley.
Rex The newts are up at Chieveley?
Sheridan Oh, you're talking about newts?
Rex Of course. (*To Austin*) Is this true?!
Austin The newts are up at Chieveley. Why, what's the problem?

Rex collapses with a moan. Barbara dashes to him

Barbara Rex! Oh, Rex!
Sheridan Can you confirm this extraordinary story?
Millichope   } (*together*) Yes.
Enid
Sheridan Carpenter!
Carpenter Sir?
Sheridan It's time we were going. (*To Tina, Millichope and Enid*) Would
    you like a lift?
Enid Pardon?
Sheridan I should hate you to be late for your own funerals.
Carpenter Ha, ha! Very good sir. Funerals! Very funny.
Sheridan Yes, thank you, Carpenter.
Millichope How kind, officer.
Tina Thank you very much.
Austin Can I come too?
Enid What?
Austin Don't argue — I'm a psychiatrist!

*Carpenter, Sheridan, Millichope, Enid, Tina and Austin exit through
door X*

Rex Barbara! Barbara! What are we going to do?

Barbara It's all right Rex — there's a newt in the bucket.
Austin Bucket?
Barbara I thought we could plant it in our pond, you see. The village pond,
I mean. Before the Inspector arrives.
Rex Barbara — you're a genius! But why is it in the cupboard?
Barbara It needed reviving.
Rex What?

Barbara gets the drugs from the first aid box and shows them to him

Barbara! This is appalling!
Barbara I was only trying to help.
Rex Help! Help!? You're the Frankenstein, Barbara, of the Amphibian
world!

Rex goes to the cupboard. Cherry and Vanessa dash to door Y and open it

Inspector Budimir enters through door Y. He carries a small box

Budimir Oh, thank you so much. I'm looking for Mr Cunningham.
Rex What?
Budimir My name is Budimir.
Barbara Who?
Budimir Of the Wildlife Commission.
Rex Oh ——
Budimir I'm sorry I'm late — but the inspection took rather longer than I
had anticipated.
Barbara Inspection?!
Rex You mean ... ?
Budimir Yes — I've scoured the village.
Rex Well, it needed a clean.
Barbara But what about Austin?
Budimir Pardon?
Rex The man who was to tell you exactly where they are.
Budimir Oh, the newts. I see. No, I'm sorry.
Barbara What?
Budimir My investigations, you see, must be conducted quite alone. I must
maintain a certain independence.
Barbara So you wouldn't be impressed if we'd caught one in a bucket.
Budimir A bucket? Dear me, no. In fact that would be quite a give away.
Rex Give away?
Budimir Yes. It has been known, you see, for people to transport these
creatures — and plant them in the vicinity before the Inspector arrives.

Barbara Really?

Budimir Oh, yes. Especially when, as your case, an area is threatened with development.

Rex Oh?

Budimir Which is why, in this instance, I had to be very rigorous. A variety of tests. Which is why it took so long.

Barbara Tests?

Budimir To be certain, you understand, that they were a long established colony.

Rex What were?

Budimir They were.

Barbara Pardon?

Budimir (*showing the box*) Your newts.

Rex (*grabbing it*) What?

Budimir Careful! Careful! These creatures are very rare!

Rex removes the lid of the box gingerly

Rex Amphibious Spangulatos!

Barbara What!?

Budimir The Greater Spangled Newt. I must take this one as evidence. But I'm sure you won't miss it. Your pond is simply swarming with them.

Rex Oh!

Barbara Then the village really is saved!

Budimir Of course. The bypass will be re-routed. It'll now go beyond the hill.

Vanessa Beyond the hill.

Budimir Yes. It shouldn't cause too much upset, locally. It'll mean, of course, the demolition of the new development — but since there's only one house up there I don't think there'll be much fuss.

Vanessa You mean ... the house on the new development will have to be pulled down?

Budimir The owner, of course, will get a handsome settlement. The mortgage paid off and a lump sum to boot.

Barbara A lump sum to boot?

Budimir Yes.

He produces a certificate and hands it to Rex

Budimir Here's your certificate. To prove you have a colony. Well, I must be off now. May I have the newt?

Rex gives the newt back

Thank you, so much. Goodbye.

Budimir exits through door Y

Barbara looks at the certificate

Barbara exits through door X

Rex Barbara?

Barbara screams, off

Barbara?

Rex exits through door Y

Cherry Vanessa!
Vanessa Cherry!
Vanessa ⎫ (*together*) I can hardly believe it!
Cherry ⎭
Vanessa My mortgage paid off!
Cherry And a lump sum, to boot!

They push the trolley back into the shower

Vanessa Is it still for sale?
Cherry What?
Vanessa Your little annexe!
Cherry Of course it's still for sale! You must move in at once!

Keith and Zandra are revealed underneath the trolley. They groan and get up

Zandra Have the guests arrived yet?
Cherry What?
Vanessa No, not yet.
Cherry Vanessa ——
Vanessa If you'd just like to wait outside ——

She shows Keith and Zandra out through door Y

Cherry We'll have to tell them it's cancelled.
Vanessa Pardon?
Cherry The party. It's off.
Vanessa Off?
Cherry Well, you can't need the money now.
Vanessa Cherry — I've got a whole new home to furnish and decorate! Of course I need the money!
Cherry What?!

Vanessa makes to the cupboard

Vanessa Now, if we can just get rid of the cricket team and the Southern Fried Chickens.
Cherry Don't open it! Don't open it!
Vanessa What?
Cherry Well, you heard what Rex said! Barbara left that newt in there. And she's pumped it full of artificial stimulants! It'll be a monster by now! An absolute monster!
Vanessa Don't be ridiculous!
Cherry Vanessa! No!

Vanessa opens the cupboard door and looks in. She freezes, with a slight squeak. She closes the door and walks to door X, perplexed

Vanessa exits through door X

Cherry Vanessa? Vanessa?

She makes to door X. There is a slight groaning from the cupboard. Cherry stops, turns back, goes to the cupboard and gingerly opens the door slightly. She peeks in and screams. She tries to close the door but it is too late

Cherry is thrown aside and the dragon costume — filled with the Chickens and the Cricketers — comes bursting out of the cupboard. Great clouds of smoke billow out as the occupants of the costume make the most terrible groaning, wailing noises. Cherry is thrown to the floor and trampled underfoot by the "giant newt" as it begins to fill the room — its jaws gaping and eyes rolling. The newt is immensely long and takes some time to get out of the cupboard (actually, of course, it's coming through the false walls). The "newt" gyrates wildly about the room finally exiting through which ever door is most convenient (perhaps it could go out through one door and come back in through another, "Conga"-like)

When the "newt" has finally gone Cherry staggers to her feet and dusts herself down. She composes herself

Cherry Vanessa!!!

Cherry exits, slamming the door behind her

Black-out

CURTAIN

FURNITURE AND PROPERTY LIST

Further dressing may be added at the director's discretion

ACT I

On stage: Full length curtains on a rail to represent shower
Trolley with curtain around it on castors (for coffin)
Cupboard (with fake back) on castors. *In it:* cricket helmet, coat
    hook, door handle
Chairs
Clothing, sports bags, towels, etc.
Mirror

Off stage: Large book (**Cherry**)
Rhinestone-studded cowgirl suit on a hanger (**Enid**)
Ten gallon hat (**Enid**)
Guitar (**Enid**)
Bright blonde, curly wig (**Enid**)
Sports bag containing cricket pads (**Austin**)
Large tin foil parcel with sandwiches, individually wrapped (**Austin**)
Plates for sandwiches (**Barbara**)
Bank notes and small change (**Vanessa**)
Coffin containing black bin bag full of mud (**Sisters**)
Newt photograph (**Rex**)
Very long pump-action screwdriver (**Tina**)
Sports bag containing PC uniform (**Keith**)
Cushions, table-cloths, etc. (**Vanessa**)
Tiny valises (**Southern Fried Chickens**)

Personal: **Austin**: keys
Millichope: very long pump-action screwdriver
Barbara: book
Darren: spectacles

ACT II

Off stage: Newt photograph (**Rex**)
Protest placards (**Protest group**)
Cricket bat (**Barbara**)
Huge dragon costume (**Bradley**)
Bag (**Bradley**)
Screwdriver (**Tina**)
Bucket (**Millichope**)
First aid box containing various bottles with potions, etc. (**Barbara**)
Small box (**Budimir**)

Personal: **Barbara**: handkerchief
Sheridan: certificate
Budimir: certificate

LIGHTING PLOT

ACT I

To open: Full stage lighting

No cues

ACT II

To open: Full stage lighting

No cues

EFFECTS PLOT

ACT I

No cues

ACT II

No cues